AF251241

Portrait of a Life

Firouzeh Razavi

Hamilton Books
A member of
The Rowman & Littlefield Publishing Group
Lanham • Boulder • New York • Toronto • Plymouth, UK

Copyright © 2011 by
Hamilton Books
4501 Forbes Boulevard
Suite 200
Lanham, Maryland 20706
Hamilton Books Acquisitions Department (301) 459-3366

Estover Road
Plymouth PL6 7PY
United Kingdom

All rights reserved
Printed in the United States of America
British Library Cataloging in Publication Information Available

Library of Congress Control Number: 2011920664
ISBN: 978-0-7618-5475-3 (paperback : alk. paper)
eISBN: 978-0-7618-5476-0

∞™ The paper used in this publication meets the minimum
requirements of American National Standard for Information
Sciences—Permanence of Paper for Printed Library Materials,
ANSI Z39.48-1992

To my mother, Masoumeh,
who has taught me to celebrate life
with a positive mindset.

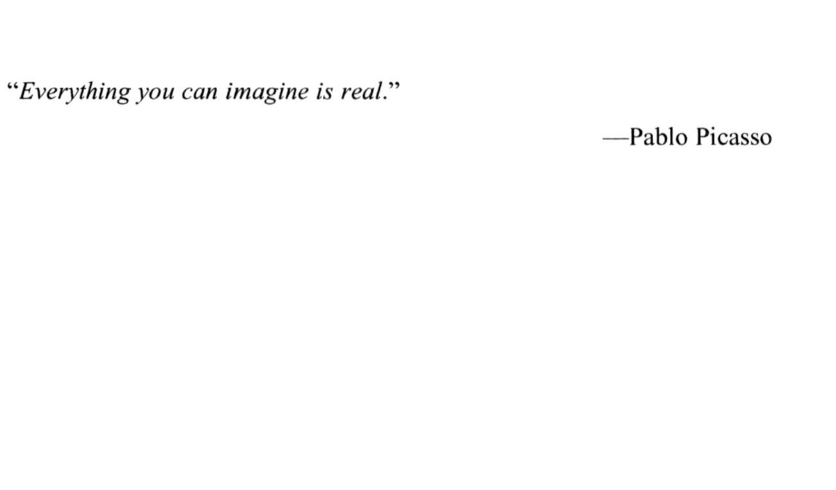

"Everything you can imagine is real."

—Pablo Picasso

Acknowledgments

I am immensely grateful to Susan Walker for reading the initial manuscript and giving valuable advice and suggestions for improvement; you are an extraordinary friend.

Thanks to Daralyn Schoenewald, Phillip Villarreal, Beeta Jalali-Ghajar and Nima Jalali-Ghajar for their editorial assistance.

I am deeply appreciative for Phillip Villarreal's assistance in helping me find a publisher for this book.

I'd like to thank Della Brosnan, Bobbi Posen, Mike Posen, David Widmer, Cecelia Wakiji, and Jo Ann Wallius for their encouragement while writing this book.

And most of all, I'll like to thank my husband, Mehrdad Jalali-Ghajar, my daughter, Beeta, and my son, Nima who have been the inspiration of my life.

This is a true story. The names of the characters have been changed to ensure privacy.

Chapter One

Who could that be?

The telephone had begun ringing just as I lay my sleeping son down in his bed. After being up all night, I feared the ringing would awaken him. I ran as fast as I could from his room to the living room and picked up the phone. On the other line was a man who introduced himself as Mr. Brolini from the Vatican Embassy in Washington D.C. I had been expecting a call from him, but not this soon. Only two days ago I had received a letter from my friend Nina that was essentially about a restoration job for the Vatican in Italy. Nina was the owner of the Monet Gallery in Santa Fe, New Mexico. In the letter, she mentioned the painting restoration project that was going on inside the Vatican, and nearing completion, they needed an additional contemporary artist to join a group of other American artists and experts. She had highly recommended me to the Vatican's art department.

From the day I got her letter until the call from Mr. Brolini, all other thoughts had come to a standstill in my head. When I received Nina's letter, I was so excited that I screamed loudly for a few seconds, making my throat hurt. I read it twice. Talk about euphoria; my life's dream had been realized. The restoration of masterpieces in the Vatican is a dream of any painter. However, for me-an Iranian artist and a Muslim woman-it was extremely exciting. This job offer was unprecedented. I was deeply honored and flattered, though somewhat discomfited. After I spoke with Mr. Brolini, I was so excited that I jumped up and down in the kitchen, singing and dancing until I heard my son cry. After the initial excitement had passed, I called my husband at work and gave him the good news. At first, he was very surprised, but soon brought to my attention all the inconveniences this job would have in our children's lives. As realization sank in, my joy led to complete disappointment; somehow, I had completely forgotten the zero chance of accepting this job.

Mr. Brolini asked to meet to discuss a job contract and getting me a visa to Italy. I told him that I needed a few days to think about the offer and to talk it over with my husband. Although in my heart I knew it would be very difficult, almost impossible, to accept the offer, I asked my husband to help me to decide.

"When Mr. Brolini called—hearing him explain the terms of the contract—my heart was beating so fast and loud that for a few seconds I could hardly speak," I told my husband. "My blood tingled hearing him say he saw some of my paintings in the Monet gallery. He told me he thinks I am an exceptional artist."

Upon hearing my emotional explanation about the conversation with Mr. Brolini, my husband said, after a long pause, that he'd go along with whatever decision I made; the decision was stitched onto me. For a short time, I felt honored to be considered to work on the restoration of the worlds most famous and beloved art treasures that somehow I completely ignored all the problems inherent in the offer.

I returned to my son's room to check on him. He had fallen back to sleep. Standing silently over his crib, I watched him sleeping very peacefully after a long bout of crying. I tiptoed and returned into the living room. I sat on the couch and for a long time I gazed at one of my paintings, thinking that never in my wildest dreams did I imagine I would be invited to go to the Vatican and work on masterpieces. I couldn't help but think a dream had come true with the job offer, but all I could really consider were my young children. My daughter was three and a half years old, and my son was only one month old. How could I leave them and my husband here? Could I take them with me to Italy for a year?

Moving would be harder. My husband had signed a one-year contract to teach at a university and had just been promoted to the manager of the research department in the company where he was working. My mother was not in the U.S. and thus couldn't help them.

As I was thinking and trying to figure out how to remove the road blocks to my future, my mother's words suddenly echoed in my head. "Luck follows one through the years, but only once may knock at the door. Be ready to open it when it knocks," she had always said.

I felt at a very strange place in my life; I was trying to be a mother, wife and artist. I spent my days taking care of my family and still trying to keep a hand on my art.

It's a hard thing growing up, even if you're 33 and counting, I thought to myself.

Only at that moment did the reality sink in that I had no chance of accepting the job. As night fell, I was still reluctant to let this chance slip away. I called my mother in Iran. She congratulated me about the job but was concerned that, if I took it, I would be away from my children for a long time. She then brought to my attention the political ramifications of a Muslim woman working for the center of Christianity. She wasn't sure what kind of reaction I would get from the Islamic government of Iran.

That phone call was the end of my wishful thinking. I was now convinced I had to turn down the job, and yet I called neither Mr. Brolini nor Nina for five days. I had a few sleepless nights. I hardly ate or did any housework. I felt completely drained. I stood in front of my easel for a long time and looked wistfully at my unfinished painting, and thought to myself there are more important things than this job—like my children, who mean the world to me. Still, I didn't want to lose this chance.

I dragged out making my decision for days even though I knew from the first day that I couldn't accept it. I knew deep down that going would be unfair to my husband and young children; still, I mourned the loss of an incredible artistic opportunity.

On the fifth day, I woke up early in the morning with my decision made. I looked around my small apartment with its walls lined with my oil paintings, watercolors and drawings and felt content. I decided to be happy no matter what might come along.

Why should I spoil any more days with worry? I asked myself.

Five long days had passed, and all that remained of my decision was calling Mr. Brolini. One telephone call marked both the sweetest and saddest of days for me.

"Mr. Brolini, I cannot accept your offer," I said, my voice catching in my throat as a thread of regret snaked through my body.

"Are you sure?" he asked plaintively. "This leaves us in a bind. We don't have another substitute. There's still time for you to change your mind."

I sighed. "I have to consider my family," I explained. "If not for them, the decision would have been easier but my children are so young and my husband just began a new position. It's not the right time for a big move."

"I understand," he said, sounding deeply disappointed.

I then called Nina and informed her of my decision. Although at first she was very disappointed, she said, "Sometimes throwing away an opportunity can be a blessing, and this can be one of those blessings for you."

Chapter Two

Nina was a close friend of mine; she was an art scholar, a curator, and a great artist herself. The first day I met her was on October 2, 1981. She owned an exclusive art gallery located two blocks from our apartment. Time after time, I had walked by this gallery and stopped to look at the paintings through the window, but never went inside. On that day, I stood at the window and pushed my face as close to the displays as I could.

My nose pressed against the store window, I heard someone say, "Hello."

I turned my head and saw Nina. I introduced myself as Azadeh and we shook hands. Looking at me thoughtfully, she asked if I were French.

"No, I am from Iran," I replied, thinking to myself that Nina was the latest in a long line to believe I was from France.

To my surprise, she quickly said, "Do you mean Persia?"

"Yes," I told her.

"Your name is beautiful," she commented, "What does it mean?"

"It means 'freedom'," I told her.

"Would you like to come in and see the rest of the paintings?" Nina asked.

"Yes!" I replied.

Looking at Nina, an old woman, slim and short with blond hair and blue eyes set in a pale face, it struck me that she was dressed from head to toe in black. At first glance, it gave me the impression she must have lost a loved one recently. She wore a black tweed suit, paired with a matching blouse and black faille slip-on shoes and a black fur hat. Nina, in that exquisite fur hat reminded me of Marlene Dietrich in *The Scarlet Empress*. She was an example of pure elegance.

I stood inside the gallery, utterly amazed by such a large collection. It was a huge, magnificent room filled with beautiful original paintings displayed in museum-like splendor. On the floor I saw an impressive Persian carpet; a room-sized Tabriz with an overall floral pattern. Two antique crystal chandeliers hung from the ceiling. At the far end of the room, was a late 19th century Louis XV-style kingwood parquetry rococo writing desk with a pair of French Regency mahogany Berger chairs. In the right corner stood a Baroque Revival carved table and on top of the table was a Tiffany bronze and peony leaded glass table lamp. On the left side of the room was a rare harp and a pair of the most beautiful Russian Empire quilted armchairs. The walls were all painted dark red and the reflection of the chandelier's lights was dazzling on the paintings.

"Everything is so beautiful," I told Nina, still looking around in amazement.

"I have seen you many times outside my gallery looking at the paintings. Are you an art lover or an art student?" Nina asked jokingly.

"I love art and I am a painter, too," I told her.

She motioned toward the carpet on the floor and said, "This carpet is from Persia."

Looking at it, I said, "It is a gorgeous carpet; in fact, one of the most beautiful carpets I have ever seen."

She proudly said, "I have another Persian carpet in the other room; its even bigger and older. Would you like to see it?"

"Sure," I said, feeling giddy at the promise of such a tour.

She guided me into the next room, asking if I was a professional artist or if my painting was merely a hobby. I paused, thoughtfully wondering how best to answer her question. I'd never before sold a painting but I didn't consider it just a hobby.

"I paint in my spare time. I've never sold a painting before," I said.

My reaction walking in to the second room was again one of awe. I saw the most astonishing collection of paintings on the walls and another huge crystal chandelier hanging from the ceiling. A pair of Regency benches had been placed by the wall and on the floor laid a large, red Persian carpet. At the far end of the room were a fine mahogany grand piano and a bench.

"Do you play piano?" I asked Nina.

"Yes," she said, "and the harp, too; I began playing both instruments at a very young age." She then motioned me toward the carpet on the floor, "This is a late 19th Century Bakshaish carpet," she stated.

"It's gorgeous," I said to her, "I have seen a similar one in a museum in Iran. Where did you get this one?"

Nina smiled and explained that one of her Persian clients, for whom she had done many appraisals and restorations, had given her the carpet. Shortly before the 1979 revolution in Iran, her client had brought out of the country many old carpets, paintings and other collectables.

Nina believed those priceless collections of literary and historic treasures belonged to the Iranian people and should have been kept in the historical museum of Iran and not in his house. Many of those items had been recently confiscated by the IRS for tax fraud and were later auctioned off in New York.

"He owed me a lot of money. A few weeks before the IRS went to his mansion in Beverly Hills, he called me and offered these two carpets as payment and I accepted his offer," Nina said.

She mentioned the name of her client and I immediately recognized his name. "He used to be one of the most influential ministers of Iran during the Mohammad Reza Shah Pahlavi regime," I told her.

Nina got very excited and quickly asked if I knew him.

"No, but I saw him many times on the news when I was living in Iran," I said.

As we returned into the first room, I noticed a pin on her coat. The truth was that the pin scared me a little because it looked so weird. It was made of gold and seed pearls, a lover's eye design, teardrop-shaped with a single ring of graduating seed pearls around a conforming gold band enclosing a potato of a blue eye. It was an unusual piece of jewelry that gave me a chilly feeling.

Back inside the first show room, she asked me a few questions as we walked around looking at different paintings. "Where did you study art?" Nina asked.

I told her that I am essentially a self-taught artist. My work consisted of paintings in watercolor and oil, and drawings in charcoal. "I have done a few originals and copied from masterpieces, too," I told Nina, adding that I'd also like to learn restoration techniques. "I am willing to pay you for lessons," I said.

As we talked more, she seemed to become very interested in my paintings. She invited me to have a cup of tea with her to continue our discussion and I gladly accepted. She went into the kitchen, and shortly after I walked over to look at one of the 16th century paintings on the wall. I listened to the soft, classical music playing throughout the gallery, and I began to smell the aroma of coffee wafting towards me.

Nina returned to the room carrying a silver tray loaded with two cups of coffee, sugar, cream and a few cookies. "I didn't have any tea, so I made coffee instead," she told me, smiling.

I sat down at a small table from which I could see the whole room and continued to survey my surroundings in fascination. She served the coffee and sat down across from me.

Sipping my coffee, I thought to myself that Nina was so kind and friendly, I felt as if I had known her for years.

Chapter Three

Nina was born in Poland. After the tragic death of her parents in a car accident, she and her twin sister, who were visiting her aunt in Paris, immigrated to the United States. She was among the first Polish who grew up in the United States in the aftermath of the Holocaust.

Nina met her husband, William, in 1945, when they studied art and researched fine art and antiquities. They married in 1953, and since his passing in November, 1973, she had been carrying on the Monet Gallery. William founded the Monet Gallery in San Marino, California in 1935, and carried on over the years in West Hollywood and downtown Los Angeles. The U.S. Treasury Department had even commissioned him to go to Washington, D.C. to evaluate some donated paintings for authenticity. He appraised many paintings from museums, as well as private and corporate collections.

At this moment, with tearful eyes, Nina said, "William was a great man and a wonderful husband. He was 77 when he died. I learned a lot from William, not only about art, but mostly about life, too."

"I am sorry that you lost your husband so soon. When we lose someone so precious to our heart, it is very difficult," I told her.

I wanted to ask if William was why she still wore all black. But eight years after his death it was unlikely, so I didn't ask her.

Nina's twin Golda, who lived in South Pasadena, was the only family she had left in the world. Wiping her tears, she said, "I'm sorry, I always get very emotional whenever I talk about my family. Sometimes I can't control myself. Now, let's talk about you."

After learning so much about Nina, I didn't mind her asking about me. She'd been so warm and open and I felt at ease telling her more about myself. "I was born in Iran, the third of four children," I told her. "Upon graduating from the College of Translation in Tehran, Iran with a bachelor's degree in English Literature in 1976, my mother, younger sister and I came to the United States. The purpose was to study business here and after graduation return to Iran. My two brothers were already in the United States when we got here.

"My father stayed and worked in Iran to support us. In 1979, I decided to permanently stay in America after the revolution that formed the Islamic Republic of Iran. That same year, I received my first master's degree in international business and the second in management in 1980.

"During the first year of my studies for a PhD, I met my husband. He was a lecturer at a university in Los Angeles. We got married in 1980 and now live in an apartment close to your gallery," I finished.

"Why didn't you study art?" Nina asked with a tone of censure in her voice.

"I always wanted to pursue a career in art, but my father, who was a mine engineer and a successful businessman, insisted that I study business. He has a lead mine in Tehran and he is exporting lead to the neighboring countries. He always thought I had the management skills to run his business when he retired," I told Nina. "To my father, art was always the least important of any other subject. He thought painting or poetry should be a hobby, not a career. My other love is poetry. I used to spend a lot of time reading and writing it. My father thought my time was too valuable to be spent writing poems or painting. Receiving numerous awards for my paintings and poetry during high school and college didn't convince him to send me to art school."

Nina listened intently as I went on to say that my fascination with painting started in early childhood. I loved to draw and often covered school books with cartoons, sceneries or sketches of classmates instead of following the lessons. Every summer, my father insisted that I take English or Economics classes instead of reading poetry books or spending all summer painting. I learned different styles of painting and spent all my savings on painting materials and poetry books.

Every time my father found me writing a poem or drawing a picture, he'd say, "Get your head out of the clouds and read the books that are useful for your future." And I'd always jest, "Too late, Father. My whole body is in the clouds now."

A sketchbook was my constant companion from the time I was seven years old. Portrait, contemporary, landscape, and abstract were among my early favorites. I was eight or nine years old when I learned that a friend's father was a painter. He was one of the greatest painters in the recent history of Iran.

I glommed on his art, showing him my sketches and ideas of abstract drawing, talking to him about them all the time. I was a force of curiosity and willfulness when it came to writing poems and learning to paint, and I knew at an early age I wanted to be a painter in a studio working with canvas and paint. At the beginning of each year, as soon as I got to school, I couldn't wait to go to art class and when the class was over, I was the last person to leave my desk. During high school and college, I always spent more time in art classes. I was happy and felt good about what I was doing.

Before I graduated from high school, I told my parents my dream of becoming a painter. My hope was ruined by the demands of my father to study Business. I was unhappy in my youth, because I felt my father denied me the deep gratification of art. I was always reluctant to hurt my father's feelings because he had the tendency to be overly sensitive and at times, vindictive.

After I graduated from high school, I told my father that I would rather go to the Tehran Art Academy than Business school. He was furious and stopped speaking to me for days.

"He told me if I chose art as my major, he would withdraw his financial support for my education," I told Nina. "Much of the tension was generated from my mother's constant advice to accept my father's wishes."

I looked at Nina and told her that I had felt a great responsibility to my father, although in my logic I couldn't find any reason to honor a person simply because they gave me life.

In my first year of college I told Mother that I was disappointed in my father and I intended to leave school unless I was allowed to change my major. She worried about the consequences of my father's reaction and begged me not to quit. When I complained about his unfairness and blamed her for unconditionally supporting his decisions, she would fiercely defend him and scold me for my lack of appreciation.

I felt it was unfair to so blindly defend him and I told her as much, but ultimately gave in to my mother to keep her at peace. As was custom in our culture at the time, my mother deferred constantly to my father and I didn't want to be the cause of quarrelling between them.

Chapter Four

"Mother constantly reminded us of our father's sacrifices," I explained to Nina. "Anytime one of us complained about him, she'd say, 'Your father is a great man who worked hard in all kinds of weather to support his family. He would wake up before four o'clock every morning in sweltering heat, heavy rain, and bitter snowfall just to keep a roof over our head and food on the family table. It is not an easy job, being in a dark mine all day. He never asked anything from you except to study."

It seemed he worked all the time yet he managed to spend a lot of time to make plans for our future on his own. "After all, your father's good decisions are more important than your immense personal satisfaction," Mother would always say. She always wanted him to talk first. "Remember, his topics of conversation and ideas are more important than yours," she'd tell us.

Mother spent her life taking care of us and others yet she was always giving more credit to Father. He was the master of the house and, as such, always exercised his will with the belief that it was out of fairness and truthfulness. We had no right to question him and his decisions. Kids in my day didn't argue with their parents, but did as they were told. I was the only child in my family who was stunned to hear this ideology from my mother. She always looked up to Father and cared for him even when she knew he was wrong. She believed a husband is the head of his household and that is the way it stood. Although Mother's intentions were good, there was a lot of underlying fear generated by the spread of his control and worry that it might lead to punishment if we did something that was not approved by him.

Aside from all that, my mother was always supportive and persuaded me to continue writing poems and painting. Over time, I came to know that she was proud of me and my work, and that was important to me, so I continued my studies. The wonder is she made everything look so easy. After graduating from high school, when I realized my father wouldn't agree with my decision, my passion for art slowly faded.

When I told Mother that my art dream was dying, she suggested I start to see other possibilities instead of trying to convince my father to let me pursue art. So I asked my father if I could choose English Literature for my bachelor's degree and Business for my master's degree. He agreed because I was able to convince him that studying English Literature would enable me to help him to better understand the terms of export and import contracts. Though I had no interest in establishing any future career in my father's business, I felt a swelling of hope that I could spend a lot of time reading and writing poems or maybe one day go to art school. In college, I participated in art competitions and won many prizes before graduating.

My mother was always interested in my talent. When I entered a series of art competitions, she continued to be very supportive, but I always felt like I had a dent in my dream. After I got married, I became a little restless and wasn't sure which way to go with art. I didn't have a focus or passion for it any more; I was kind of lost about it.

"As an artist, I felt a little bit unfulfilled and spent my free time reading poems and literature books," I said.

A customer entered the gallery and we stopped our conversation. We got up, and on my way out, Nina asked for my phone number and much to my surprise, she volunteered to give me the restoration lesson at no charge. She also asked me to bring a few samples of my paintings to the gallery so she could see my work. I told her I would gladly bring in the samples soon.

After almost two hours of talking, I left the gallery. I felt very comfortable talking to Nina about such personal matters. She was a great listener and it felt like we had been friends for longer.

Chapter Five

Nina had charmed me and I was very eager to go back and see her again. The next day, I called her around noon at the gallery to make an appointment. Around two o'clock, I took four of my paintings to the gallery. That day, she was dressed all in black again. I was very curious to know why but again, I didn't ask.

After looking carefully at all my paintings, I realized she kept coming back to one, staring at it. It was a portrait of a man named Dr. Mohammad Mossadegh who was once the Prime Minster of Iran.

Dr. Mossadegh was almost 70 years old when he was named Prime Minster of Iran, on April 28, 1951, by the Majles, the Iranian Parliament, during Mohammad Reza Shah Pahlavi's regime. Mossadegh was well-loved by the Iranian people because he was an honest, natural leader who greatly reformed the country from kingdom monopoly and corruption. Mossadegh was opposed to foreign intervention in Iran and nationalized Iran's oil industry, which had been under British control since 1913. He was removed as Prime Minister in 1953 during a coup that was orchestrated jointly by the United States' CIA and its British counterpart, the SIS. Mossadegh was imprisoned for three years, and then put under house arrest in his family's village, Ahmadabad near Tehran, until his death.

Nina was knowledgeable about Dr. Mossadegh. Looking again at the painting, she reflectively remarked that she saw a picture of Dr. Mossadegh on the cover of Time magazine in 1951, when he was named Man of the Year.

Our conversation turned to the Iran-Iraq War, which at the time, was going strong between the two countries. Nina asserted, "I hate war. I think any war is a foolish thing. To witness women losing their husbands and sons, children losing their fathers, countries losing scientists, poets, leaders, it's just intolerable."

"Imagine if the leaders of the world united and worked as one for the people," I vehemently declared.

Nina's eyes filled with tears. "You're right," she said, "Leaders who promote war are the lowest form of humans. The people end up paying the expense at a cost of not just money, but human life. War is ugly, painful, and nonsensical. War hungry leaders believe they gain liberty through war, but they don't realize that when the people are peaceful, they grow hope. Unless they have hope, they cannot live in harmony."

Nina stood there for a minute, thinking. "The world today needs art and love more than anything else," she said slowly. In her eyes, I can see she really meant it. "If Hitler had continued art throughout his adulthood, who knows, maybe the world would be different today. Art is the best way to influence the people. Not war."

I looked down for a brief moment because for the first time, I strongly disagreed with her. Not about the world needing art, but about Hitler. "He would have been a fascist with or without being admitted to the Vienna Academy of Art," I said resolutely. I concluded with the reminder that the people of Germany were complicit, because when the Nazis first began to come into power, they did nothing to stop them. If the people of Germany hadn't had the constant goal of the overemphasis on self, Hitler would never have come to power.

"Thank God there was only one real civilization in Europe during those years, and that was France. I admired their spirit," she responded.

"It is all about how people think about war and how to learn from it," I continued.

"We need leaders like Dr. Mossadegh and Gandhi," Nina said amiably.

We stood there in the gallery for some time, discussing Dr. Mossadegh, war, and the influence of oil and Islam in the country. I left thinking again of Nina and how she was so friendly and worldly. I found myself anxious to return to the gallery and her conversation.

Chapter Six

Nina became so interested in my artwork that not only did she offer to display my paintings in her gallery, she asked me to paint a portrait for one of her customers. "It is to be a portrait of a young girl, the only daughter of a friend," Nina told me. "The girl, Pearl, was killed in a car accident. The parents gave me their favorite photo of her and want it to be painted into a portrait. Are you interested?"

"I have to see the photo first," I replied.

Nina stood up and walked to her desk to get the photograph. "My friend loves all kinds of paintings. They collect them, too. Perhaps if she likes your work, there'll be more business opportunities with her."

Opening a desk drawer, she grabbed the photo and told me how much it meant to her personally. She seemed sure that I could paint Pearl's portrait better than any other artist. As she walked back to where I was sitting, she paused for a few seconds to wipe the tears falling from her face. "What a beautiful girl," she said wistfully, looking at the photograph. "She died so young. Only 18 years old. What a tragedy."

She handed the photo to me. I looked at it, seeing a beautiful young woman with a pale face and black hair. I was struck by the resemblance to my childhood friend Ziba, who died a few months after I moved to the United States. Looking closer at the photo, Pearl's resemblance to Ziba brought chills to my body.

I didn't want to paint Pearl's portrait. I don't know what came over me, but I stared at the photo and tried to find a good excuse not to accept my first job offer as a painter. "What size do they want the portrait to be?" I asked.

"Large. Maybe 30"x40" or 40"x50"."

"Wow! That is big. I've never painted a portrait that large."

"Would it be difficult for you to paint it that size?"

"I don't think so, but I prefer to start with the smaller sizes," I said.

She explained, "Two other artists had painted Pearl, but the parents didn't like the portraits. They thought they were too serious, that they didn't fully capture Pearl's beauty and character."

I felt even more uncomfortable about the job after hearing this from Nina. "So why do you think they would like my work?" I asked.

She smiled and said, "Honestly, there is no guarantee but we can at least try and see what happens. To tell you the truth, I think somehow the parents do not want to accept the fact that she is dead. Both paintings were excellently done but there wasn't much I could do to convince the parents."

"Do they keep the portraits? What happened to them?" I asked curiously.

"The artists kept them. The parents pay the full price even though they don't take them. They are very wealthy." She then remarked, "They are so wealthy, they can afford as many portraits as they want until one of the paintings satisfies their mind."

I sat there silently for several minutes, thinking about the family. They might be difficult clients to please. Even though I had never been commissioned to paint anything before, I felt I shouldn't accept Nina's offer. I worried at refusing the offer.

"I find this sort of job an irresistible challenge but to be honest with you, knowing ahead of time there is a strong possibility of the customer being dissatisfied, I'm having a hard time accepting," I told Nina slowly.

I thought Nina would be disappointed in my decisions, but she was very understanding. "It's not a problem, Azadeh. I had guessed you might not be the kind of artist to work just for the money," she said kindly.

After leaving the gallery, I drove directly to the art store, feeling an intense urgency to paint. I felt as if I were over the moon. *Nobody but family has really seen my work before. Now many people in Nina's gallery will see it*, I thought to myself.

I rolled up the windows in my car and turned up the radio. I started singing as loudly as I could, and made a decision to try new painting styles and learn more techniques from Nina. My dedication to my old dream of being a painter was renewed as if it were a lotus emerging in the spring from a winter mood.

Nina's encouragement covered me like a blanket; I felt warmed by her compliments. As I walked around the art store, choosing new painting supplies, I realized that I had been abandoning my talent for years. I put one more brush in my basket and walked toward the checkout stand, determined to pursue my passions.

Chapter Seven

Soon we developed a routine of meeting at the gallery nearly every day. I spent most of my spare time there, helping with the restoration of masterpieces and learning different techniques. As time passed, I felt an emotional connection with Nina that only strengthened each time I saw her. The gallery became my fountain of delight. I was constantly learning about art as well as about Nina. She was someone I connected with on an artistic level, something I didn't get from other people. The gallery had become an escape for me when I needed it.

Nina taught me the importance of art conservation and I quickly learned that restoration is not simple; like varnish, oil paint changes as it ages. In fact, restoration is harder than starting a new painting from a sketch. Nina showed me different pictures of famous American and European paintings before and after restoration. I learned how to clean the varnish from a painting: a painstaking removal of the yellowed coating which forms naturally from oil based paint. I learned how to repair cracks and tears in the paint and how to correct uneven residues from past restorations or botched repairs from an earlier era. Restoration, to me, became magical; it brings a new twinkle to old masterpieces.

As months went by, my halted passion became fired up by Nina's daily encouraging words. Not only had my passion for poetry and painting been renewed, I started to see life in a different way.

I felt connected to Nina. She was down to earth, direct, and very amiable. She was very thoughtful and her mastery of the history and religious influence of art was unbelievable. Despite an age difference of 36 years, she and I became close friends. I worshiped her talent and knowledge. We had a great deal in common: We both loved art, we both enjoyed talking about religion, and we both had a love of history and learning about different cultures.

Nina seemed to have a confidence that she took for granted. Her love for art and helping others was limitless. Each time I fired off art questions, she'd answer them with as much passion as a single human being could muster. She also actively supported charities, especially children and art organizations. She believed there is a spark of art in every child's mind that should be fanned into fire by teaching them art. Once when one of her favorite charities was investigated for financial corruption, she was very irritated that the news had slowed down people's contributions to other charities.

"People have the right not to trust some charities. Unfortunately, some people take advantage of other people's willingness to give," I told her.

"There is nothing more visceral than cynicism, nothing more brutish than greed," she said her brow wrinkling as her voice lowered in frustration.

Chapter Eight

Nina and I spent countless hours together painting, laughing, and sipping tea. It was as if we had rediscovered our inner children. The Huntington Library, in the city of San Marino was one of our favorite places to visit. We went there many times for her research and studied in its private library. The more time I spent with Nina, the more I was amazed at how active she was. As far as I could tell, the only time Nina slowed down was when she slept, which was never more than five or six hours a night.

As time passed, I noted that one thing never changed about her. She always showed up dressed in a 1910-1920 era hat regardless of the weather and she always wore all black clothing. I finally found the courage to ask why she wore all black clothing and a vintage hat all the time.

"Hats relieve depression," she laughingly told me. "To some people, old clothes are just old clothes, but to me they are memories." I noticed she did not fully answer my question and I didn't have the courage to ask again.

Nina worked 10 to 12 hours a day, almost everyday. She came to the gallery as early as six o'clock every morning and painted, worked and taught restoration and art all day, then helped charities in her spare time. I marveled that she could work so feverishly at such an old age.

Some days we worked for so long, she would just collapse on the couch at the gallery and fall asleep. She'd wake up a short while later, and jump back into a painting, a restoration project, or delve back in to a report for the museum.

"How can you continue to be so active day after day?" I asked in astonishment.

"For two reasons: keeping a regular routine and pursuing art. Each keeps my soul alive," she said, smiling.

Nina truly was a furnace, constantly stoking herself on to the next project and fanning life into everyone. She volunteered to visit, drive, prepare meals and assist elderly people in need through programs like Meals on Wheels. Many holidays, she visited children in the hospital, delivering gifts, playing the piano or harp, and reading books to the sick children. She thought music was the best therapy for ill children and adults. Retirement was not an option for her.

She always emphasized to all of her students to give something back to society and to be mindful of others. She made it clear that she felt it was everyone's duty to serve the community in one way or another.

"You are a superhero," I'd say to her.

Nina laughed. "Giving back to others does not make me a superhero."

I remember that period vividly. Her emphasis on the importance of art in people's life was always so strong; it was as if she felt it should be the only thing in life. Every time I heard her stress the importance of art in schools, or tell students they should learn about collections, I wondered what my father would think of her viewpoint.

Chapter Nine

The first Thanksgiving after Nina and I met, she asked me to help her make Christmas ornaments for a charity. Her project during Christmas was to make angels and the Nativity scenery. She would then donate them to charities that would sell them and use the money to help poor children learn music and art.

Some people are motivated by money, fame, or power and some just want to show off their talent, but what motivated Nina was the self-satisfaction she felt in helping a good cause. I was thrilled she had asked me to join her. We sat alongside each other, laughing and making the ornaments. She made things so much fun. I was always delighted by her passion, and I learned a lot about art in those days.

The first year we started making ornaments, we began on a Friday, the day after Thanksgiving in 1981. I remember it so vividly because it had rained steadily for days, and it was still raining that morning when I went in to the gallery at seven in the morning. Before we started working on ornaments, she always first played the piano, then the harp.

"Listening to music grows our imagination and inspires us. It will lift our souls. It teaches our minds and touches our hearts, and most of all brings excitement to the brain," she would say every time before we started to work on anything.

After playing two or three songs, we would then go to the workbench and sit down to paint the ornaments. We'd sit there for hours, chatting and painting away the day.

Weaving our memories, we talked about the most unforgettable events of our childhood, the decisions and the friends who influenced us most in our lives and in our art. We talked about our family, the people in our lives and our relationships with them. We both believed those people had made us into the people we are.

On that first rainy day, I asked Nina how her Thanksgiving had been.

"I spent all day with my sister at my house. I cooked turkey, baked a cake and set up a nice table. I played music, but none of my efforts could bring her to cheer," she said sadly with worried eyes. "To be honest, I had a terrible time with Golda."

Chapter Ten

Golda and Nina were born in Poland in 1916. As well as being identical twins, they were also their parent's only children. Their mother was a gorgeous, elegant woman, and a gifted opera singer. She always dressed Nina and Golda alike. Friends and relatives often confused them, even their father. But even though they were dressed alike, Nina and Golda were emotionally very different.

They didn't have a happy childhood; in fact, they had a terrible life growing up in Poland. Their parents quarreled over almost everything and made their home a hell. "Even as children, we hated to go to the park or on trips with our parents," Nina said with a grimace.

The two felt deep loneliness and the only way Nina felt any sanctuary was when she played the piano or the harp. One day, she begged her father to send them to Paris where her great aunt lived. Her father agreed and while some thought his decision was foolhardy, her mother was thankful because she saw the effect their fighting had on the girls' mental and physical health.

"When we arrived in Paris, I took a deep breath and looked around, like a prisoner who catches a glimpse of blue sky from the confines of the prison yard," Nina said, her face lighting up at the memory.

"Finally living in peace, I spent a lot of time studying and playing music in Paris," Nina continued. "I began to reinvent my life through art while my parents had fought furiously over our custody after getting a divorce. One day, when my uncle accompanied my parents to the attorney's office, his car crashed into a truck and both of my parents died instantly," she finished, a tear slipping down her face.

The news of their parents' death had a profound psychological effect on Golda. She buried her hurt but it began to surface as she and Nina reached adulthood.

"She never came to terms with our childhood. Never grieved for it, never moved on," Nina said.

Nina and Golda were adopted by their great aunt and uncle. They stayed in France for two years before immigrating to the United States when life became more difficult for Jews in Europe.

At 14, they started high school in California. Nina took lessons to learn German and Russian, and by the time she was in her 20s, she could speak five languages fluently. "I studied art and worked at a few museums until I met my William. We married when I was 36," Nina told me. They never had children.

Golda married a charming Italian doctor, the love of her life. They were instantly besotted with each other. He was crazy about Golda, and she loved him beyond reason. It was from Golda's husband that Nina learned to speak Italian.

Golda's happiness was short lived. Signs of trouble began to appear on the horizon. She became an obsessive shopper, living in lavish debt. Differences and disagreements began to pile up and the two drifted apart. John, Golda's husband, began working late and sleeping in his office. He also began sleeping with his young secretary.

Golda was horrified when she found out, had a hysterical fit, and they got divorced. Golda went into a severe depression and lost all interest in life when he married the secretary a year later. She never really socialized or married again. Deeply hurt, she cried all the time and lost interest in everything she and Nina had once enjoyed together.

"Golda is the only family I have left in the world. If anything happened to her, I think I would die, too," Nina said pensively.

"Although Golda and I are identical twins and we have the same DNA, we often don't act alike or think alike. From our early childhood, I realized that she is very sensitive and hardly adaptable to big changes in life."

"Did she ever get any psychological help or treatment?" I asked. I was curious at the difference between the two sisters. Nina seemed so strong; it was hard to imagine her twin as anything but.

"Yes," Nina answered, "Golda is under the treatment of one of the world's most prominent psychologists in the field of depression. The problem with my sister is that she is very dependent on me now. She feels very lonely. She is self-consumed with triumphs and failures, engrossed in her own inner drama. I feel that simply being busy and aware of what is happening right now without wishing it was different is the foundation of a healthy mind. But unfortunately my sister doesn't think that way and she never listens to my advice or even her doctor. She even went on antidepressants, but nothing seems to help."

"Maybe her depression was deeper than her husband's betrayal," I suggested, trying to find the reason. "She lost her parents at a young age, she left her homeland without them when you moved to France, and again, you two moved to the United States. That's a lot of change for any one person to handle. She must have had a hard time fitting in," I said, truly understanding Golda's situation.

Nina disagreed, saying Golda's depression was due to her weak mind and an inability to forgive and forget. "It is not a social identity problem. She just can't distinguish between the trivial and the important memories in her life," Nina said. "We all have bad memories, but dealing with them, controlling them, is essential to our health, don't you think?"

"When I left Iran and came to America, I had a difficult time adjusting. I missed my family, friends, and homeland. Shortly after coming here, I heard my best childhood friend had died suddenly. Emotionally, I was in deep trouble. I couldn't bear the combination of pain and fear of the new changes in my life, but soon I learned to protect my soul; I had to adapt to all the changes in my life and move on accordingly. Depression is a strong dam to happiness," I explained passionately. "But how can we put aside our bad memories? Our minds and memories make us who we are." I paused, and then asked if there were no other treatments available for Golda's depression.

"Electrical shock is the last thing we haven't tried. I really don't want her to have that. I've heard it's very painful," Nina said.

I winced.

"Nothing has changed for Golda. She's gotten worse, if anything. I really think that it's all in her mind, that her physical pain is just a mirror, but when I tell her that, she gets very upset and calls me selfish," Nina continued.

"Not everyone has the strength to face such turbulences in life," I said, disagreeing with Nina's diagnosis.

"True, but if the person is not willing to change their mind, nothing else can be done. Every time I see Golda I ask her why she persists in her anger, hatred and self-loathing. But she is stubborn."

"Seems like your sister's brain is broken," I said. "You have to help her find the means to fix it." I thought about Golda for a minute, wondering what really triggered her feelings.

"Why don't you two live together?" I asked. "It might help ease her depression."

"Although we are twins, we have two very distinct personalities," Nina said, smiling gently. "I am very active and I can't stand to see someone sit around all day and do nothing. That's what she does every day. I just don't think I could live with her."

Nina sat quietly for some time, gathering her thoughts. Her face tightened in worry. After getting lost in her thoughts for several minutes, she finally said she believed that people must reinvent themselves time and time again as they rise from the past.

"Our humanity should be continually renewing itself as we overcome disappointments and move on from them. We are shaped and formed by the things we love, but Golda truly seems to have no love for anything except unhappiness!"

"What does Golda do with her time?" I asked.

"Nothing worthwhile. All day, she sits around the house, thinking and talking about the past. Sometimes she stares at the TV for hours, watching the same programs over and over. She does not have any passions in life, not for sports, or art, or anything. She calls me a workaholic, but once asked how she could be more like me."

"What did you tell her?" I asked quickly, marveling that identical twins could be so different from each other.

Nina chuckled and settled into her chair. Picking up a cup of tea, she said, "I told her I don't just sit around thinking of my ambitions, I am always working to make them happen. I don't spend all day watching TV, I'm always volunteering for good causes, learning new things or working.

"I have helped make a difference in so many people's lives, but not my sister's. I try not to be selfish. I try not to live in fear. But now I spend all day worrying about Golda, wondering if I should leave work and help or if I should just ignore her. I have wasted days and days of my life for her, and the terrible thing is that has made her dependent on me," Nina finished.

My heart broke for Nina and her sister. There seemed no choice for Nina but to continue caring however she could for Golda. Their relationship reminded me of Ziba, a friend I had growing up who also faced stark challenges.

"Nina," I asked, "doesn't Golda have any children or friends to keep her company while you are busy?"

"No," she replied. "Except for me, she doesn't have anyone. We are both childless."

"That must be so hard for her not to have a child, a friend, or a companion."

"I know, but to tell you the truth, it is our parents' fault. They didn't allow her to have friends when we were growing up. She grew up lonely and dependent on my mother to occupy her days. My only hope for her now is God."

"Is she religious?" I asked, still amazed Golda had no one to turn to.

"Yes. From an early age, she was very religious."

"Did her spiritual beliefs help her?" I asked her.

"Yes, they did, and I am praying to God that He will help her get through her depression now."

I was totally absorbed in Nina's story and was surprised to feel relief knowing that Golda was religious, that she read the Torah on a near daily basis. *At least she has that*, I thought to myself.

"If the Torah brings her happiness, by all means, she should use it," I told her. "Although I am not religious, I have seen the effect faith has on the mind. I believe it helps divert negative thoughts into hope," I told her, thinking of my childhood friend Ziba who was blind from the time she was born. Ziba had used her faith and religion to change her despair at her disability into hope for a happier life.

"Growing up, I had a friend who showed me the power of faith," I told Nina, voicing aloud my thoughts of Ziba.

Chapter Eleven

I first met Ziba on my ninth birthday. It was a day unlike any other. The night before was very cold and windy. I woke up early, still tired after not sleeping well. I stepped down from my bed, feeling dizzy, and walking like a zombie, I went into the living room. I felt excruciating pain in my back, sharp reminders of the shots I had gotten there three days ago.

Two weeks before my birthday, I'd suddenly felt extremely ill in class. I was burning up with a fever by the time my mother came to get me from the principal's office. I had a severe headache and even worse neck pain. My mother rushed me to the doctor thinking I had the flu. Instead, the doctor diagnosed me with meningitis. None of my friends were allowed near me. I could only talk to them on the phone.

That day in the doctor's office, I screamed my heart out the entire time the doctor gave me a shot in my spine. When I complained of severe pain, my mother would remind me how lucky I was to have been diagnosed so quickly.

"Otherwise, you'd have been in the hospital for days," she kept telling me.

My mother is a kind, thoughtful woman with a wonderful personality. She always lectured me to be selfless. "There are always people worse off than you. Things could have always been more difficult. Make the best of what you have, make it count and appreciate every moment," she always told me in a strong, steady voice, like a preacher who speaks with purpose.

I was missing my friends dearly in the two weeks that had passed since I was forced to leave school. I shivered the whole way to the living room. I quickly turned around and retrieved a blanket from my room.

I returned to the living room and lay down on the couch, the blanket covering my body. I looked at the big living room window covered with steam from the heat. I walked toward the window and with my finger, drew a small bird on the glass. The bird disappeared from view as I exhaled on the window.

I sketched the bird again and again as I listened to my parents talking in the kitchen. I overheard my father telling my mother that she would have to take me to the doctor by herself that afternoon.

"I just hope it doesn't rain or snow," my mother said, sounding disappointed.

I went back to the couch to lie down; quietly looking through the window I'd drawn birds on. My mother and father came in to the room singing "Tavalodet Mobarak", the Persian Happy Birthday song.

I smiled when I saw the large gift in my mother's hands, having forgotten that it was my birthday. "Good morning," I croaked in a weak voice. She sat next to me and handed me the gift. Father rested his hand lightly on my forehead and asked how I was feeling.

"You look much better today," he said.

My eyes glued to the gift box, I asked what was inside. "Something I am sure you will use for a long time," my mother said.

I held the box up, examining all angles. I admired the wrapping, a beautiful turquoise paper hugged by a shiny white ribbon and topped with a beautiful artificial butterfly. I was very excited. I leaned forward and paused. I hesitated to open the gift, but slowly pulled the ribbon. The butterfly fell off, tumbling to the floor. I continued to open the gift: a painting set complete with a canvas, a few tubes of oil paint, a few brushes and some varnish.

I hugged my parents and then looked through the set as if I had just found a treasure chest. My father left the room, returning with a tall wrapped gift. It was a black easel. The color surprised me.

"I hope you will create masterpieces with this set," my mother said.

I was filled with delight, eager to start painting.

"Working on your school lessons is more important," my father admonished, as if he had read my thoughts.

My face fell. *Why give me the easel if he didn't want me to make use of it?* I wondered.

My mother just smiled and told me to paint whenever I felt the urge. I don't know how my mother convinced my father to buy that gift, but I felt very excited and happy. "I don't want to spoil your joy, but you need to rest," Mother told me. "We have a doctor's appointment this afternoon."

"Do we have to go?" I asked, looking longingly at the painting set.

"Yes, but it won't take long," my mother replied.

It was half past four in the afternoon when we left the doctor's office. The visit was short and Mother was pleased to hear that we wouldn't have to go back again. I was pleased to hear I didn't have to get another painful shot.

It was cold, dark and dreary outside, and our taxi had not arrived. We waited on the sidewalk for several minutes before my mother said the driver should have been there by the time we got out of the doctor's office.

"I told him to be here thirty minutes early! He should have been here ten minutes ago," my mother said impatiently. "I told him to be here thirty minutes early!"

Fifteen minutes passed and standing there, I felt very sick and cold. My head was pounding and my back felt like it was breaking. I looked at my mother, who looked as impatient as I felt. I saw the frustration cascading from her face like a fountain. I leaned on an old telephone pole, and looked at the sky.

"He's coming!" my mother cried.

The taxi pulled over and I dropped my mother's hand I'd been holding to stay warm. We jumped in the car and warmth began to imbue my body. Mother gave our home address to the driver and he merged into the heavy traffic.

Five minutes into the trip, I felt very dizzy and sick to my stomach; I felt nauseous. I grabbed my mother's hand and told her I felt like I was going to throw up.

She looked at me anxiously and said, "Breathe deeply. Try to relax."

I rested my head on her lap and closed my eyes, trying to divert my thoughts by thinking about something else. A few minutes passed and I felt a little better.

The driver chatted with my mother, talking about the unusually cold weather, his long hours, and how he was overburdened by skyrocketing food and oil prices. At first I listened, but soon the conversation didn't interest me and I stopped paying attention. I wished he'd stop talking. I opened my eyes every once in a while, looking at my mother's kind face and wished I could be like her one day. She was raising four children—two girls and two boys—without much help from my father. I thought how that couldn't be an easy task. I asked my mother if we were close to home.

"Yes, we're almost there, dear," she said gently. I closed my eyes again, hoping for the quiet to linger, but the silence didn't last long. The taxi driver kept chatting, telling my mother he hoped the snow wouldn't continue to fall because he didn't carry snow chains in his taxi.

I opened my eyes and watched the snowfall. As always, I got very excited. I sat up straight, leaned over the door and watched a big flake of snow glide across the window. Soon I noticed the heavy snow coming down faster. Minute by minute the snow fell faster. My eyes grew tired from watching the snow fall. I sensed trouble and delay ahead and began to worry.

The falling snow became heavier. The streets' lamps came on all of a sudden. Snow continued to flurry from the sky and the wind blew faster, slapping the face of everything in its path. All the snow meant that the drive to our home, which sat on top of a hill, would be treacherous. The driver was caught off guard by the sudden shift in weather and kept changing his speed, unsure of what to do next. He seemed confused, and as he kept plowing through the snow, the windshield wipers swiped more furiously across the windshield.

His actions were making me nervous. Soon, I too started to show signs of discomfort and began to cry silent tears of frustration. The cab driver slowly pulled over to the side of the street and stopped.

"I can no longer drive in these conditions. You need to walk home. It's not that far," he said apologetically.

What a heartless man, I thought to myself. We got out of the car, stood there on the side walk, freezing to our bones, afraid of the slippery road, trying to decide what to do next. For a short moment, we stared at each other. The neighborhood gradually emptied out.

"It's best just to walk home as fast as we can. We are very close," Mother said, taking an umbrella out of her purse and snapping it open. We headed home as the snow fall turned into a raging blizzard that paralyzed the city. I stopped, refusing to walk any longer.

"I can't go on," I told my mom. "I feel sick."

She motioned towards the road and kindly said, "We are very close to home. Can't you see all the cars on the street are stranded?"

I kept crying and told her I was dying and she should find a car to take us home. She grabbed my hands and said patiently, "We shouldn't stop, dear. If we wait here any longer, we'll both catch a cold."

The pavement was wet and very slippery, and what few cars and people there were in the streets, were in a hurry. We saw other drivers with tire chains chugging through the snow. The air was getting colder. I stopped again after we'd gone a while up the street.

"I'm dying, Mother. I'm freezing. I can't go on," I complained.

Looking at me straight in the eye, she said, "Please, let's just walk home." I felt empathy for her and started to walk again. Frustrated, I told her that I wished she could feel my pain.

Passionately, she said, "Believe me, Azadeh, I do. But there is nothing else I can do." She stopped and removed her gloves. She grabbed my icy fingers and started to rub them. I felt warmth burst into my hands.

"You should realize we don't have any other choice but to walk home, so instead of focusing on cold and pain, just think about getting home," she said. We began walking again and she started her usual lecture, telling me to be thankful it didn't start to snow earlier or we'd have longer to walk.

I cut her off with a rude, "Yeah, our situation could be much worse. You are always saying that." Tasting bitter discomfort, we kept walking.

Feeling the cold breeze numbing my skin, my teeth began to chatter. I couldn't make them stop. My head felt heavy. My mother said something to me but I didn't catch it because I had just noticed two people walking at the end of the street. They weren't far from us and I noticed they weren't carrying an umbrella.

"Do you see those people coming toward us? Why are they walking so slowly?" I asked. Mother peered down the street and said, "Maybe they are afraid of slipping."

"No, it seems they are having a problem," I said. We moved steadily toward them. When we got closer, I saw that it was a young woman and a child approaching us. I felt that something was not right as the distance between us grew shorter and shorter. We paused for a second to look at them, but were unable to see through the darkness of night and snow.

Suddenly, Mother let out a cry of recognition. "It's Sima and her daughter Ziba," she said. "Ziba is blind," she leaned down to whisper in to my ear.

We lived in a small town called Shemiran, north of Tehran, where everyone knew one another and were friends, but I had never met nor heard about them. Now I could see both Sima and Ziba up close. I forgot my pain and the cold air, and focused my attention on Sima, who was clutching her daughter's hand.

"Hello Sima, how are you?" my mother asked.

"I am fine, Mrs. Javadi, but why are you walking in this heavy snow?" Mother hurriedly explained what happened with the taxi driver. Sima told us that they were headed home from her work when the blizzard began. We kept the conversation short because it was so cold, and began walking home.

After we'd gone forward a few steps, I paused and turned around to look at Sima and Ziba again. Suddenly, my mother lost her balance and fell to the ground. She fell flat in a pile of snow, face down on the sidewalk. At first, we both laughed but I quickly realized she was unable to move her legs. I tried to help her stand up but I couldn't. I called loudly for help. Sima, just a few steps back, ran towards us, leaving Ziba behind.

Sima reached out her hands and slowly pulled Mother up. We both helped her to wipe the snow from her clothes. She thanked Sima but she still couldn't walk normally. She had injured her knees and was in great pain. I looked out at Ziba, who was standing helpless in the sidewalk, alone and mute with fear.

I walked up to her and reached for her hands. At first, she thought I was her mother but I told her it was me. She wasn't wearing any gloves and her fingers felt as cold as ice. The brisk cold air had colored her cheeks a brilliant blood red. I wasn't sure what else to say or do; I just stood there with her and watched Mother and Sima talk. Mother motioned for me to return with Ziba where she and Sima stood. Ziba asked what had happened.

"My mother fell down. I think we need to help her get home. She can't walk by herself," I told her.

As I held Ziba's hand, my mother's voice echoed in my head: "There are people always worse off than us." I suddenly realized for the first time in my life what my mother meant.

Ziba and I reached Sima and my mother and we all headed toward my home.

Chapter Twelve

Mother opened the front door and turned the lights on. We stamped the snow from our feet as we entered the house. Mother went into the kitchen to get an ice pack for her knee. She helped Ziba into a seat by the fireplace before sitting down in a nearby chair. We were all grateful we'd reached the house, where the air was warm and pleasant. I could see Sima and Ziba clearly from my perch, and I took the opportunity to study Ziba's pale face. Her cheeks were still pink from the cold and her hair was jet black. She was dressed in a dark blue raincoat that covered her from the neck down. She even wore black canvas shoes. I was struck by the color of Ziba's eyeballs. They were as white as a cloud, motionless and scary. I had heard about blind people but had never seen one up close. Her face was sweet and fair. Regardless of her unseeing, empty eyes, I thought she was very beautiful.

Mother offered them tea and cookies but Sima said they weren't hungry. I sat there quietly, unable to take my eyes off of Ziba. Deep in my heart, I felt sympathy for her. I didn't say a word, just sat next to Ziba and watched her. Once Sima stood up to leave, I offered my gloves to Ziba and tried to put them on her hands.

"They're very warm. What color are they?" she asked in a low voice.

"They are green," I replied.

"Green like grass or green like a new leaf?"

"Green like grass," I replied. *What does it matter what color the gloves are? She can't see them*, I wondered to myself.

They walked out of the house, my curious stare following them down the sidewalk. Closing the door, I bombarded Mother with the many questions that were running through my head: "When did Ziba become blind? How did it happen? Why are her eyes that color?"

At first, Mother was reluctant to answer my questions. She said I needed to rest first. She would tell me about them later, she said. I was so curious I could not wait any longer; I insisted and Mother sighed. My mother explained that Ziba was nine years old and was born blind. Her father had been a bread maker in downtown Shemiran. He and Ziba's older brother were killed in a bus accident when Ziba was just four years old. Sima and Ziba live in poverty in a tiny, primitive room behind an old house. They were destitute but too proud to ask anyone for help, so they continued to live in desperation.

"Thank God Sima is well liked in the neighborhood," my mother said somberly. "She cleans houses around here and some people are helping them out.

"Poor thing," Mother continued, "she has to take Ziba with her everywhere: to work everyday, to the store, anywhere. She is tireless, and even with all the misfortune in their lives, Sima and Ziba live happily together."

"Is Ziba going to school?" I asked curiously.

"No, there isn't any school for blind children here. Even if there was one, I doubt her uncle would let her go there. He's very controlling, and he's a hardcore fundamentalist."

My mother paused for a moment after this, and looked thoughtful. I knew she would bring up her usual lecture. Sure enough, she said, "Thank God some people are so generous, otherwise Ziba and her mother would be in a much worse situation."

This comment seemed like nonsense to me. *Why would God let Sima and Ziba suffer so badly and where was God when all these bad things happened to them? Why didn't God help them?* I thought to myself.

Mother's description of Ziba's life was like a punch to my face. It hurt to think of how unfairly she and her mother had been treated by God. Imagine my disappointment when I found out about their life story and all that suffering.

Still reeling, I asked her why God couldn't help them.

"God sent us all here to help each other. It is not his duty. It is ours. Sometimes life's cruel hands hold us powerless and helpless. There's nothing we can do about it except to make the best of whatever God has given us."

I thought Mother's words made sense; still, a seed of doubt was planted in my mind. It was the first time I grew a serious doubt about God's fairness. I was uncomfortable about the sudden contradiction in beliefs. Skepticism took root in my mind at nine years old, and questions would pile in my mind as I grew older.

I couldn't bear to continue the conversation and told my mother I wasn't feeling well. "I should go lie down," I told her.

"Good idea," she said. "We had a long day. You should rest now, but don't forget to thank God for sending Sima to help us tonight."

I went to my room, my mind overloaded with many thoughts. I closed the bedroom door behind me, and paused for a minute. I could hear my mother's voice echoing in my head: *There are others worse off than us. Things could have been worse, but bless God that it wasn't.*

I was exhausted. I threw myself on the bed, and staring above me at the white ceiling, I felt a strange tapping coming from my heart. I wasn't sure if it was because of my illness, or if it was pity for Ziba and her mother.

What could be worse for them? I thought. My heart was hurting for them, I wanted to help in anyway I possibly could. *I'll talk to God tonight in secret once everyone goes to bed*, I decided.

After supper, I skipped dessert and hustled back to my room. I sat in there for some time, and I channeled my disappointment into action, drawing something new. I sat at the new black easel with my painting kit nearby. My thoughts flew out of my head and onto the easel.

Before long, Father peeked in the doorway and said sternly, "Azadeh, it's time for bed." I sighed because I still had a long way to go on my drawing. Once in bed, I tried to sleep all the while thinking to myself that I should wake up early the next morning to work on the painting. Shortly, Mother came into the room to check on me.

She turned to leave and I sat up in the bed. "I just can't sleep!" I exclaimed. "Mother, are you sure God exists?" I asked quickly, before she could leave.

"What kind of question is that?" Mother remarked. "Of course God exists."

"Do you think God is just?" I implored.

"Of course." Mother replied.

"Does God love everyone?"

She opened her mouth to answer, but before she could, I interrupted her with another question.

"If God does exist, why was Ziba born blind? Why would God give her family so much misery?"

Mother despised these questions and gave me the answer I knew she would: "God tries us through suffering and pain. If our ultimate goal is to grow, learn, and discover things about ourselves and about God, then unfortunately a life of ease is probably not the way to get there."

Mother looked exhausted and held up a hand at me when she saw I was ready to continue my line of questioning. "God works in mysterious ways," she said resolutely. "All I know is, God made us all different and he loves us all."

I wasn't ready to end there. I showered her with more questions.

"How does death spread throughout the world? Why do so many die from starvation? How did hunger sweep Africa? How does death penetrate dreams?"

Mother was out of patience. Her smile slipped a little as she said, "We can't blame God for all the suffering on the planet; it's the evildoers. It's not God's fault."

I couldn't believe God would let people suffer if God really existed. "I don't believe God exists," I said decisively. My mother, who already looked fed up with my cynical questions, became exasperated when I said this.

"Laa ilaaha illa llaah! There is no God but Allah! Your talk is getting insulting, Azadeh, and you will perhaps regret it some day. Never say that again, and for God's sake, hold your tongue about God's existence," she said in a firm, calm voice that was full of religious fervor.

She had never before spoken to me like that. My heart fell as I realized I'd upset my mother. I worried that I had disappointed her with my belief. "I'm sorry to upset you," I said quietly.

She sat down beside me and patting my hair gently, said, "Be sure that the existence of God is a sure thing. The world won't rest without believing in God. Please, stop disarming your faith whenever you see disabled, terminally ill or poor people."

I still wasn't convinced. This was Mother's way of persuading me religion wasn't a farce.

Mother, who was trying not to show her disappointment in my divine line of questioning, kissed me on my forehead. While leaving the room, she asked why I was so reluctant to believe in God. "Can't you just trust me when I say God exists?"

"Mother, do you think God is a he or a she?"

"It doesn't matter if God is a he or a she. The point is that you believe God exists," she said wearily. "If you open the door to your heart and let God in, you will see how blessed you are."

She helped me into bed, still lecturing.

"We are all created by God and are bound by religion; doubt draws us to the ground. No matter when or where man's life on earth has started, it is formed by fate that has nothing to do with God's fairness."

I pondered her words, thinking of Ziba and Sima. *Where does fate come from then?* I wondering, still worrying about my new friend's blindness and poverty.

"Life is a short journey. Not everyone gets on the same path others do. If we focus only on those who have less, peace would be upon us. The only thing we must do is help the disadvantaged instead of wondering about God's intentions," she continued as she tucked in my blankets.

I felt weary after such a deep conversation. I still could not agree with my mother but I didn't want to argue anymore. "I got your point, Mother. Good night."

She walked toward the door and said in a honeyed whisper, "Without faith, your life is unwitting. It is time you realize what is happening, and what the impact will be, if you don't believe in God."

Before turning the lights off she added, "To save your soul, believe in God and the divine justice. It keeps you pure and free from sin and you can go to Heaven."

She smiled, said good night, and closed the door.

Chapter Thirteen

I lay there for several minutes after my mother left the room. I struggled to believe what she always preached. She always told us that hope cannot exist without faith in God.

Her reasoning didn't make sense to me. I felt a strong desire to come to a fuller understanding of religion and why it was needed to be moral and fully appreciate life. But lying there in my bed, I was very tired and didn't want to think about it anymore. I closed my eyes and went to sleep.

The next day, I woke up late. I felt much better that morning. All night, I thought a lot about Ziba and Sima. Not one detail of their faces or their clothes escaped me. I stood under the window gazing at our garden. I always loved waking up after the first great snow. I saw trees with patches of fresh snow on their branches and icicles hanging from the roofs; perfection was everywhere. The snow melted soundlessly. It was white and spotless every-where. The streets were covered in snow for days. We heard on the radio that all schools, due to the deep snow, were closed for the day. The sun appeared and was soon veiled by clouds, and ruined the perfect picture I had in mind for a painting.

After eating breakfast, I returned to my room, studying peacefulness and maintaining a quiet mind. I felt a creative urge swell and got up to continue the painting I'd started the night before. I was hoping I could pull myself to-gether to finish the painting before the day ended. I had always found painting and writing poems relaxing ways to escape from stress. It was such a pleasur-able way to spend a snowy winter day.

My younger sister and I used to have tea parties with our dolls but very soon, I outgrew playing with dolls. They went into my toy box when I picked up my first brush. I used to time myself when I was painting to see how fast I could finish a painting. Poetry and painting always conveyed my sorrow or bliss, therefore timing the process gave me firepower. I've always taken 20 deep breaths for relaxation before I started a drawing. Often I was thinking about the subject of my next painting while working to finish the first. That morning, I was very weak and tired and I could barely keep my eyes open but I kept right on painting for hours.

Around noon, Mother came into my room holding a small plate with slices of fruit. I stopped drawing. She left the tray on top of a small table in the room and asked what I was painting.

I covered the drawing with my hands and said, "Please, don't look at it. I am not done yet." I was usually very protective of my paintings, not letting anyone see them until they were done.

She smiled and said, "I can't wait to see it, but you should rest more. Don't overwork today." She left the room. I felt a great hurry to finish the painting; I kept on, and hours later, I finished it.

I left the painting on the easel and went into the living room. I lay down on the couch and enjoyed the silky silence. Minutes passed as I listened to my mother talking on the phone with someone. The window was covered by steam from her cooking in the kitchen. I went and stood at the window. I lifted my hand to draw something on the glass but I changed my mind. I gazed at the beautiful pines covered with the fresh snow outside in the yard. Mother came into the room holding a glass of water and my medicine. She handed both to me, and after I swallowed the pills, I told her I had finished the painting. Eagerly, she asked me if she might see it.

Holding hands, we walked toward my room. Before I opened the door, I asked Mother to close her eyes. I guided her into the room and sat her down on the chair in front of the easel. I told her to open her eyes and she did. I couldn't wait for her to beam at me and give me approval. Instead, she looked at the painting and paused.

I wrung my hands nervously, afraid she didn't like the piece into which I'd poured my heart. "This is very different," she said, her face void of any excitement or emotion.

I said, "The subject is my own idea." I always could tell by her expression whether she liked my paintings.

She smiled and said, "Why did you choose to use only black and white colors?"

Concerned, I said, "Don't you like it? I worked all this morning to finish it."

She hesitated. She took another long look at it and replied, "Of course I like it, but I see a forceful and imaginative expression in it. Honestly, I am not that crazy about the subject, especially the dark colors."

I was very surprised to hear Mother, who had always praised my every little artwork as a masterpiece, say she wasn't crazy about the subject.

I had painted a winter scene: the sky was veiled with black clouds, and a long empty street had many trees on both sides of the road, all covered in snow. Two black roses rested in the middle of the street.

Mother hesitated and said, "I have never seen any black roses. Why did you choose such dark colors?"

"This is how I express my thoughts," I explained, wondering why she didn't understand. "You may dislike the colors in the painting but the emotion of the artist selects the colors. I didn't choose the subject, the feelings in my heart and my mind did."

"What are you trying to express?" She questioned, looking at me with curiosity.

"I am trying to go beyond reality to paint from life. I want to use the reality of life as a source of inspiration and stimulation," I said. "I feel it helps put me in touch with my deepest feelings. Painting is about thoughts and decision making and interprets what the artist feels from what she sees. When I am happy, or sad, or angry, or bitter, these moods become part of my painting," I said with a slight tone of anger.

"I honestly think when you are not feeling well you should not rush to paint," she said.

I felt exasperated. I felt frustration and replied, "I paint or write poems because I want to give expression to my feelings. How am I supposed to give utterance to my thoughts if I choose only colors that are satisfying the viewers?" I argued. "When I painted this scene today, I was fuming about Ziba's situation, fervently thinking, what has she done wrong to be born blind?"

"You should paint or write poems when your mind is alert and eager," she advised. "It is only then your imagination will blossom with beautiful subjects and cheerful words. When you are tired, or sick, or sad, you shouldn't paint because sometimes the result may not be as satisfying as you want it to be."

I disagreed with her, saying the best paintings in the world had been painted by the artists when their emotions were stirred up.

"It is up to you. I am not an artist nor am I a good judge. I just gave you my honest opinion." She stood up and left the room.

I rested for a while after she left, thinking to myself that I would write that letter to God that night. I wanted to ask God what He was thinking when He brought Ziba into this world, blind and with nothing to hope for.

Later that night at dinner, I asked Father for his permission to invite Ziba to our house. He right away said yes, which was surprising because he disliked our friends coming over, and when there were guests, he didn't always make them feel welcome. Television was fairly new in Iran when I was growing up and only a few families in the neighborhood owned one. Anytime Mother had our friends come over to watch television, he would shout from the table to my mother, "Have these children no home of their own?"

When he gave permission for Ziba to come over to our house, I thought to myself that it was out of sympathy, but I was very thrilled, thinking and planning how to spend the time with Ziba. Because I didn't have that many choices, I decided to wait and figure it out when she got there.

That night before bed, I started to write my letter to God. Step by step, I went over my questions, frankly and thoughtfully; they were the questions I had in mind for quite some time. For me as a nine-year-old, God's inequality in creation was no ordinary question which I would automatically accept along with my mother's imperfect and divine analysis. I finished my letter and hid it inside the drawer of my desk.

Chapter Fourteen

The next morning Sima brought Ziba to our house. I immediately guided her to my room. At first, I wasn't comfortable with her, and asked Ziba what she usually does with other friends when they get together. To my surprise, she told me she never had any friends; that she spent all the time with her mother when she cleaned houses, and sometimes played with a small cat at one of the homes her mother cleaned.

"I guess you could say the cat is my only friend," Ziba said somewhat sullenly.

To have no friends at this age sounded very sad and odd to me. When I talked about my friends, school and teachers, she listened in unparalleled awe.

After lunch, I began telling her about my painting and poetry. I noticed she was very interested to know more about art and music.

I was so excited to have someone to listen and discuss art with. I read a few of my poems to her. When I described the subject of my latest painting, she became tremendously enthusiastic about art. She asked me how I became a self-taught painter. She also wanted to learn to draw. The more I talked about art, the more her curiosity began to fill, eventually overflowing her learning veins.

I've never seen anyone as eager to learn as she was. I was charmed by her easy manner and insight. I was in awe of her complete lack of self-pity; she was happy with her life despite being blind and poor.

Though I was initially convinced I would be bored having Ziba over, the morning hours flew by, and by the afternoon, we'd discovered we had a lot in common. I realized we could be good friends. I had never met anyone like her. She was a weary pilgrim, a day traveler with a burning thirst for knowledge, especially when it came to poetry.

Nearly immediately, I recognized her as possessing an artist's mind. Despite her poor and miserable upbringing, she was blessed with the gift of poetry.

I recall, two weeks after I met Ziba, Mother had arranged a late ninth birthday party for me. I remember it was on a beautiful Friday. On that day, everyone, except Sara, came to our house on time. Sara, as usual, arrived late. Sara was my childhood friend. She was a beautiful girl with long black hair, brown eyes, a dazzling set of white teeth and a fair face. We were in the same grade and went to the same school. She was talkative and possessed with the idea that she must express herself on every subject and every occasion.

She lived in a big, old mansion that was the most expensive house in our neighborhood and was very close to ours. We were living in a neighborhood with a big gap between rich and poor. Her mother and mine were good old friends. I grew up among rich, blessed kids but Sara was the richest. Her family had factories, farms and buildings all over Iran. She was an only child and had been spoiled by lenient parents.

Growing up in the 1960s, our extended family and Sara's would get together on Fridays, the weekend and holiday in Muslim countries. We kids would play hide-and-seek, jump rope, games or sometimes we girls would play with make-up.

Sara had a habit of showing up late to every birthday party, and she used to bring the most expensive gift to show off. As we grew older, I realized how giving expensive gifts had become her way to buy off friends, and I deplored this trait in her the most. Once when we were asking each other who were our superheroes, I remember Sara said that her parents were her superheroes because their superpower was spending.

Although she'd go to the store with her parents on a shopping trip almost every week, she always preferred to go with her grandparents, because she'd say, "They don't know the meaning of the word no!" She had many dolls, but she always begged for the biggest doll in the store. Sara didn't like to play with most of her toys; she just wanted to have them. She'd always go into great detail about the things, such as toys, jewelry and clothes that she had bought recently.

I remember on that day, Mother had heaped all my birthday presents on the living room table and sat down with me and the guests as I opened them. I sat at the head of the table and I explored my cornucopia of goodies.

While opening each present, Sara asked the person who had brought the gift, "This is beautiful! Where did you buy it? I want to buy one for myself." Anything my friends and I would get, she'd wish she could have one just like it. Sara was famous as the Queen of Spoilers.

While I was busy opening my birthday gifts, Father entered the living room. To my surprise, he'd brought Ziba with him to our house. I had not invited Ziba to the party, fearing she would feel uncomfortable with my friends. I was glad to see her nonetheless. Ziba held a bunch of red-pink roses that were covered by a newspaper, and seemed they had been cut from a garden. As Father introduced Ziba to my friends, I gladly stood up and went to her, got the flowers from her hand, kissed her on cheek and thanked her. I told her how happy I was to see her. With a sweet smile, Ziba wished me a happy birthday. I helped her to sit down on a chair next to me.

As I was kindly talking to Ziba, I saw Sara's face. She was laughing quietly as if she were making fun of Ziba's gift. Somehow, Sara's jealousy had resurfaced. Frustrated by her inability to get attention, looking unhappy and impatient, she demanded I continue opening the rest of the presents. She, right away, gave me the gift that she had brought for me.

When I opened Sara's gift, I remember everyone said, "Wow!" She had given me a gilded, heart-shaped, angel locket suspended from an expandable chain, with an 18K-gold closure in a beautiful, black-leather, jewelry box. Sara looked satisfied and proud when everyone kept on remarking how gorgeous the gift was.

On that day, I wanted Ziba to participate in everything we did, but I noticed most of my friends were not comfortable with her presence because they couldn't play their usual games. In the yard I watched my friends play jump rope, hide-and-seek and swing. I felt very sad that Ziba couldn't do any of that. The thing that struck me the most was when Sara kept on rolling her eyes every time I said we cannot play hide-and-seek or watch TV.

Soon, I realized that in everything we did, Sara treated Ziba as a pitiful token. Her careless words had something in them so menacing that they accentuated the bitterness of wrong. Sara had no balance between right and wrong. For example, every time she talked to Ziba or asked her questions, she'd say it so loudly as if Ziba were deaf too! Ziba railed against the "pity-based tactics" of the people around her. She was a proud person, and she truly believed that if you are raised barefoot and poor, you could still move up in life's line, past children of the rich and upper class, no matter what gender, race or other problems, as long as you possess a strong will.

"I am poor and blind, but I can be anything because I have the will and I'm not lazy," she'd say every time she felt pity from others.

Sara's behavior was disgusting to soul and heart. As a shaken shadow, it was intolerable and it dismayed me, as it did my other friends. Looking at them, I thought, *These are only privileged kids who have everything in their lives—yet, they are still unsatisfied and get bored quickly.*

I remember that day vividly because I didn't have a pleasant experience. My other friends' dissatisfaction tore our pleasures in everything we did. Yet still, Ziba seemed to know the use of patience, and helped me go through that long day. Gradually, I found out that she was one of the most interesting, intelligent and compassionate persons that I've ever met; she didn't have any trouble knowing how to love or be loved.

As time passed, Ziba got to know my friends as well, but I sensed that she didn't like Sara. Ziba was self-contained and independent from her surroundings. She was a person who did not depend on others for her existence. Ziba's gifted art of composing poems was soon noticed by an anguished Sara, which stooped her to jealousy. Something about Sara that never changed and bothered me a lot was her jealousy. Every time she came to my house and saw Ziba spending time with me, she was visibly upset. I found her whole expression and demeanor disturbing. Sometimes with her childish gestures, she'd emphasize her objection of Ziba being there. Each time she saw us together, she twitched her skin like a cat who feels a flea. To me, Sara was a Queen of Pain and Ziba, a Queen of Contentment.

One day in 10th grade, when we were in Literature class, I heard Sara reading one of Ziba's poems that I had kept in a folder in my room, presenting it as her own. I was furious and choked with anger at her dishonesty. I felt her character seemed to be at an end. I remember the teacher liked the poem so much that not only did she say that it was the best poem, but asked her to reread it. What was striking was how she exceeded the teacher's expectations and got the highest grade. I recall after class, I confronted Sara in the school hallway. Shaking my head in dismay, I told her that she ought to be ashamed of herself to cheat like that. I told her exactly what I thought of her, "You are a cheater. That poem is Ziba's. How can you steal it from her?" To my surprise, not only was she not embarrassed, but she also denied stealing Ziba's poem.

Sara swore to God that it was hers. For a person who had lazy language, it was hard to believe that the poem was written by her. I also told her how much I was disappointed with her action and her inability to think for herself.

As if nothing was going through her mind or through her ears, my words were going in one ear and out the other; she started talking at the top of her voice and making lots of gestures. Sara had been known by others as having a short fuse. She went on to tell me that I was just jealous of her talent and that a blind person could never write those kinds of verses. I stopped arguing with her because I knew she always had a justification for her wrongdoing, as if she had no mental consciousness. Many times she even believed her own lies herself. For a moment I thought I should return to the class and tell the teacher or go to the principal's office. I thought Sara should have been punished, but later felt sorry for her. I thought she was a person with a lost soul, dangerously coupled with boundless wealth and never-ending wishes. Yet despite having it all, she felt miserable most of the time. I changed my mind about going to the principal. What bothered me the most was that she was only upset because I had found out about her plagiarism.

When I got home I told Mother, but surprisingly she said that I had done the right thing. "Success at school starts at home," she said. Mother told me that she didn't recall if Sara had ever received a scolding for her irresponsible behavior or cheating from her parents.

I didn't tell Ziba about this. What would it matter if she knew? Ziba always thought too much privilege would spoil some people. In regards to Sara, she had told me, "Sara has a privileged life. She has so much, yet she's unhappy. That brings sympathy to me." We thought that no matter how much Sara got in life, she wouldn't be happy. "Some people have everything they want; they have experienced everything life has to offer with supreme comfort and security. Then they reach a stage where they can no longer enjoy anything, because there is nothing left to desire. They end up on the ultimate trail of misery and depression," Ziba had said.

As time passed, Ziba and I met weekly and spent a lot of time together. Ziba was always telling me how much she loved coming to my house. It set her at ease and gave her a sense of self, she would always say.

Of course, we didn't agree on everything but argued peacefully, with precise and decent thought. The one topic which we disagreed on the most was God and religion. Ziba was very religious, and although she loved art, she was most passionate in expressing her feelings through spiritual poems. Poetry soon became her nourishment, as if it was a sanctuary for her soul.

Our friendship grew as thick as a tree, its roots embedded in a mutual love of art. Her eyes lit up in pleasure every time I read any poems or literature books to her. Looking into those eyes, I marveled that I had ever thought them frightful and scary. Sometimes I had to read a book twice because she liked it so much. Ziba always listened attentively. Whenever I read to her, I could see her ears sharpen, waiting to pick out and capture new words. Shortly after picking up a new word, she'd compose a great poem, wanting me to write her verses down on a piece of paper.

Nothing gave me more pleasure than the sound of her reciting a new poem out loud. Using simple but insightful language, her poems were plain but had something in them so divinely sweet that it filled the air with the truthfulness of her feelings. They made me rediscover the bright freshness of creation in my own paintings. As time passed, I wondered how these amazing poems flowed in significant amounts from the mind of a person with the disability she had, especially considering her cold, cramped living conditions. I constantly wondered where her poetry came from.

How can she have such visual language when she can't even see? I would wonder. *How does she interpret what she can't see into beautiful lyrics?*

She had never seen a mountain, the sky, the sea, flowers or nature, but she knew what they looked like. She told me her soul had been filled with art and poetry, giving her hope when there was nothing to see but her imagination. Poetry had become Ziba's ultimate companion, and I, warmed by her words, began to experiment with new styles of painting and was thrilled by the results.

When Ziba turned 11, I asked my mother to buy her a tape recorder for her birthday. Ziba loved it. She had often told me how difficult it was to memorize all the verses that came to her instantaneously. She called it her "poetic pillow."

From then, week after week, she would give me her taped poems to transcribe into a notebook. Listening to her voice on the tapes, putting her words in writing, always amazed me anew to her ability. I was puzzled by her perception and wondered if she wasn't really blind.

Though we always disagreed on the topic, Ziba and I discussed religion time and time again. She was always telling me that if it weren't for her faith in God, she wouldn't be able to go on with her disability in life. She made the choice not to blame God for her blindness and poverty; she had chosen to be happy despite those setbacks.

I once asked her why she thought God, if he truly existed, would allow some people to be born disabled and disadvantaged. "I never really thought about that," she told me. "I think I am blind because of bad luck. I don't think it's God's fault. There is no armor against fate. People who ask God for all their wishes to come true rarely enjoy life. I am happy with whatever God grants me."

Chapter Fifteen

As time went by, I had a feeling something was wrong in Ziba's life, but I didn't want to bring it up with her. One day as I was working on transcribing her poems, I noticed despair in her words. When I finally brought it up with her, she at first said nothing was wrong. I insisted otherwise, and she finally admitted her uncle was making her life difficult.

I had never met him, but I knew from my mother that his name was Rahmat, and that he was a truck driver. He paid for Ziba and Sima's food and housing each month. Ziba had once told me she and her mother were dependent on his help.

My mother told me Rahmat was raised by a father who had reveled in traditional Islamic polygamy and had had two wives. He was the seventh child of nine children; all were raised with a religious fever that, for Rahmat, had grown much more complex as he grew older. He was always telling Ziba and her mother that things were too tight and they should conserve food.

Ziba said not a day went by that her uncle didn't yell at her, call her ugly, blind and useless. He even told her she couldn't eat because she didn't work. Rahmat took control of their lives after the death of Ziba's father and soon after fell in love with Sima even though he already had a wife and four children. He resented Ziba, convinced that if it weren't for her, he could have taken Sima as his second wife. He had beaten Sima several times for refusing to send Ziba to a government-run orphanage.

My bones turned to water hearing this about Rahmat. I couldn't bear to hear any more about a man with such a mean soul. I told Ziba that we should do something about it, but to my surprise she suddenly panicked and got very nervous. She started to cry and begged me not to tell anyone. I told her I couldn't simply squeeze my eyes shut to these abuses and hope they would go away. "If I continue to do that," I told her, "by the time I open my eyes, you will have had great injuries." Ziba said she could never see me again if I told anyone.

She was always very scared of uncertainty, believing that this secret, once spilled like water on the ground, could never be gathered together again, leaving her to live with a lifelong disaster. Through it all, she never wanted people to feel sorry for her. I was furious with her uncle and felt bad for Ziba. Nevertheless, I calmed down and promised not to tell anyone.

Ziba told me Rahmat was a devout Muslim who often said religion was more important than national identity and that he would hurt anyone who didn't respect Islam. Hearing more about him, I got scared too. I promised again to keep it all secret. Two days passed and having known about the abuse was a heavy weight on my shoulders.

I couldn't keep the secret any longer. On the third night at dinner I told my parents. Although they expressed their strongest condemnation and sympathy, they told me that it was a matter between Ziba's family and that my family shouldn't get involved. I didn't want Rahmat around Ziba and her mother and asked my father if there was something legal we could do.

"No, not in this society!" my father said.

Mother said, "Knowing Rahmat, they need a miracle from God now." I was shocked they now knew about the abuse but weren't willing to take any action. I was disgusted.

Month after month passed and it was a miserable time for Ziba. I was hoping that someone would see the abuse and intervene. My parents watched closely and did what they could to help them financially.

Gradually I learned more about Rahmat. I once heard from a neighbor that he thought those who spoke against Islam should be beheaded. He still didn't allow Sima to clean the homes of Jewish people, though the pay was better. He had even told them to avoid walking by the homes of Jewish and Bahai people. Although Ziba had described him as a cruel and selfish man, she also felt it wasn't his fault. I deeply disagreed. She blamed his childhood, the conditions and the environment in which he grew up. I argued that cruelness was a result of his nature. To me, there was just no excuse for abuse.

The abuse had been private for years to the point of secrecy, and Ziba still wanted to keep it a secret. These miseries were exacerbated by the other hardship of her uncle's abuse, yet Ziba remained calm in the face of cruelty. If anything, her uncle had grown more ruthless and she would get mad at him, but always said she didn't dislike him, just his actions.

As his mistreatment grew, I was disheartened, grieving almost, and thoroughly enraged by the injustices of life. I always expressed my doubts about his religious beliefs, wondering how a religious person could pray to God yet to be so hurtful and inhuman.

To me, the most mystical thing about Ziba was with life's many turbulences, she was still positive and calm, even in the midst of the chaos and turmoil in her life. She always argued that the fundamental asset of humanity is to have capacity to endure misfortune and injustice.

We talked a lot about Rahmat. I wanted to explore his inner humanity, often asking myself, and Ziba, if people like him turned violent because of self-love or self-hate.

During my high school years, Ziba told me many times that poetry filled her soul with hope. One afternoon, Sara and I went to visit Ziba at her house. When she opened the door, we saw bruises on her face and her arms. Sara and I were both angered when Ziba told us Rahmat had beaten her after catching her recording poems on the tape recorder. He told her to never write poetry again. I was furious. I wanted her to report him to the authorities but Ziba was adamant that it would do no good. I wanted to stay at her house until her uncle returned home and confront him. I felt talking with him might be a good first step, but I was wrong. Ziba begged us to leave and not get involved. She felt hopeful and said she didn't want to sit on the sidelines of life complaining or asking for help just because she looked frail and was disabled.

I felt awful. I should have understood better and helped Ziba by giving her hope she could overcome her situation, rather than questioning her intentions and criticizing her.

Walking back home, Sara and I discussed the situation. Sara thought that Ziba was a fearful person who didn't have the courage to stand up for herself. I thought she was just trying to avoid conflict as much as possible. Sara thought that perhaps Ziba had been inflating her claims about her uncle's mistreatments. I disagreed, telling Sara that Ziba should be peddling her story to anyone who would listen to get help. Sara changed the subject, looking bored. For her, if a problem didn't affect her personally, it might as well not exist.

As time passed, Ziba's insight grew, and she continued to compose poems full of love. With each breath, she blasted impossibility. Her words were full of hope, inspired by wonder and delight in the beauty of being. This was one of my favorite poems:

> Doors to Happiness
> Fellow travelers,
> In the chamber of life,
> The light of God is still shining.
> In sickness and in health,
> I am here on the earth,
> Hang on and hope,

For better or for worse,
I am here with hope.
Keep the faith-it is heaven on earth.
"Why?" you ask,
Keep the faith, you do count on earth.

Ziba awakened in me an awareness of the beauty of happier subjects for my paintings. When spring came, we'd spend Persian New Year together. She'd bring her birdsongs, blasting the tape outside our garden, hoping to teach the birds, once again, to sing as if they were flying above a mountain. She had this notion that widespread urban noise pollution meant that birds couldn't hear each other any more, and consequently, they were failing to learn songs from each other as they once did. She truly believed there was a chance the birds could really sing instead of bleeping, rasping and squawking. She also taught me how to close my eyes and ears to the chaos of any event around me and imagine in my mind each of the birds and listening to their song. In this way, I could forget any pain and concentrate on the positive things in my life, like some kind of mediation. When I tried this technique, I learned that is the best way to meditate.

Chapter Sixteen

It was in March 1964, that I came up with the idea to take Ziba with us to our vacation home in the Alborz Mountains. I was excited to tell Ziba she would get to "see" a whole new world just a few hours away from us.

While my brothers and sister were packing clothes, games and toys, I was packing poetry and literature books and my painting materials. It was tremendously exciting for all of us to wake up early to go on a trip.

I was too excited to sleep the night before we left. All night long, I rowed ideas for different activities in my head, vividly imagining the breathtakingly beautiful mountain sceneries, gold cup flowers in the fields and the old village.

We left the day before New Year. We got up early in the morning, before dawn, and we packed up the sky blue Chevy with supplies. We were leaving for 13 days, seven of us squeezed into the car for the ride. We left around 5 a.m. to pick up Ziba then headed out of the city. After an hour, the sun began to rise as we reached a winding road leading to the top of a hill.

Sometimes during the trip, my father would tell jokes and everyone would laugh, even though we'd heard the jokes many times before. I described every wondrous sight to Ziba along the way: the dark, lordly pines, the singing bluebirds, and the majestic sky. She listened, as always, very carefully. My brothers and sister kept asking me to be quiet; they were bored by my admiration of nature.

As far back as I can remember, every time we drove anywhere on a long trip, my parents told us entertaining stories of their childhoods. As we kept on driving, we all became restless and asked to stop for a break. Miles passed and we became more and more antsy; there were no rest stops in sight. Father, who had a consuming passion for traveling unlikely paths, noticed a narrow, one-way, unpaved road that looked interesting.

All of a sudden Mother told him to pull over. We all asked where the bathroom was. When she pointed to the bushes, Ziba, my sister and I all said, "Oh, no, we can't! How could we possibly 'go' behind the bushes?"

In the end, we had no choice but to give in to nature. When Father tried to go back, he realized there wasn't enough room to turn around. We kids were screaming in thrilled terror while Mother looked very uneasy. We could have been killed, and except Mother, we were all excited and laughing.

I still don't understand how Father turned the car around. We thought he was a hero, driving those narrow roads while cars and buses honked and spit fumes. It was not an easy task. Sometimes it seemed as if civility on those roads was in short supply with cars coming straight at us, in our lane, driving the wrong way because it was shorter or easier or perhaps because the drivers were sleepy or confused.

Father drove us slowly through the villages so we could see the market places. Shops on both sides sold flowers, fruits, nuts and colorful rugs. As we picked our way through every alley and yard, I took a deep breath, holding it as long as I could and letting it out slowly so I could get the full aroma of the village.

A few minutes later, we reached the house. It burst like a brilliant poppy from the green field. Ali, who served as our gardener and housekeeper, was running after an errant sheep while a barking dog chased them both. Ali's wife, Akram, cheerfully opened the iron gate and welcomed us. The house was two stories and had two bedrooms, a living room, a bath, a kitchen, a huge porch and sat on a rocky ledge in the middle of several acres of land and garden. Ali had built raised bed behind the house where he grew a variety of vegetables and a fenced-in garden in front of the house was filled with herbs.

As soon as we entered the house, I immediately guided Ziba into the garden, which was surrounded by rolling green lawns and a panorama of plants and flowers extending as far as the eye could see. I saw the most dramatic display of blooming flowers, their fragrance flowing through the light breeze. We walked and I delightfully described the scene to Ziba. For both of us lovers of nature, the idea of a rustic backyard retreat was the ultimate fantasy; a place to write poems and get away from stress. She was enjoying my admiration for the lotus, which I particularly enjoyed because its blossoms rise pure and untilled from mud; I thought it was a symbol of a person like Ziba, incorruptible from desolation. Each journey is as good as the destination, but this trip, this vacation was different because, for the first time, we had a friend join us.

As I held her hand and we walked around the garden, I described all the sights to Ziba: The garden filled with narcissi, bright lipstick-pink tulips, colorful hyacinth, golden daffodils planted in sweeping drifts beneath a fine apple tree that showed off an old stone wall. The colorful pansy and violas stole my heart, and Ziba's by proxy, with their inquisitive whiskery faces. The blossoms of the trees filled the air with perfume and floated down to cover the ground and pond with a soft pink and white blanket. Croaking frogs lurked around the pond edge and fish flapped their tails on the surface. Every time we came to the vacation house the first thing we'd tell Ali is that his garden was a reproduction of heaven.

I continued to describe my personal version of paradise to Ziba, thinking what a pleasure it was to be there with her, breathing in the fresh and fragrant mountain air. In my heart, I was disappointed she couldn't see the scenes I tried my best to describe. Ziba particularly loved the smell of apple blossoms, so I'd pick her a few but felt guilty because then they wouldn't make apples. We knew how to entertain ourselves, and our imaginations required no batteries and few props. We discussed how to bring unexpected beauty, color, and landscape with succulent plants to our verses and my paintings later.

We saw Ali in the garden. I asked him to identify the flowers we had collected. With two gold teeth in front, he smiled and for the next hour, he taught us about the plants and I took notes as we walked around the garden with him. My brothers and sister joined us shortly after.

We were all interested in everything we saw: birds, insects, fish and geology-but especially the plants. I made drawings in my note pad, some crude sketches, and some delicate doodles that were both loving and precise.

We loved Ali and he loved us kids. At night when he wasn't busy, he'd play the flute and sing Turkish songs for us. Although we couldn't understand a word of Turkish, we enjoyed his music. I told Ziba that Ali was an amateur botanist and an avid gardener as well as a Koran teacher in the village mosque. He had the greenest thumbs I had ever seen.

Everyday around noon when he came to rest, Ali would be tired and dirty, but he was very happy. Ali was always very proud and delighted when we complimented him and he wanted very much to pass his knowledge to us. If weather permitted we'd go for a tour around the garden. Having a captivated audience, Ali would show off his beautiful flowers, plants, animals, chickens, sheep, and chicks. Sometimes he'd treat us to fruits from his trees: juicy oranges and tangerines, even apples.

We had planned on going to the lake that day but soon after we had lunch—shish kabobs cooked with fresh herbs and vegetables from the garden—the weather suddenly changed and light rain started to fall and continued all afternoon. For the briefest instant, before there was any sound, a web of electricity flickered across the garden and then came lightning.

We were very disappointed in the weather, but Mother promised to take us to the lake the next day. I watched mournfully through the window, hoping the rain would stop and describing the downfall to Ziba. Later that afternoon, the rain stopped but it was very windy. All the children including my two brothers, my sister, Ziba and Ali's 10-year-old son wrote wishes on pieces of colored paper and tied them to a tree so the wind could carry them to the sky. It was Mother's idea. She believed that maybe, just maybe, the wind would take our wishes all the way to the sky.

The sudden storm had knocked out the electricity. Mother sat on a stool in the living room, trying to be useful by holding a strong flashlight above us as we each wrote our wishes. Ziba whispered hers into my ear and I wrote it down for her, every word sinking deep in my heart: "God, please grow love in my uncle's vacant heart so Mother and I can live in peace."

While writing these words, I asked myself, *How can a small heart be able to attribute this much forgiveness to a brutal man? How is she able to live under that much anguish, yet ask God for his forgiveness instead of his punishment?*

Years would go by before we learned that after we'd all gone to sleep that night, Mother had sneaked outside to read our wishes, hoping to help make them come true. The next morning was the first day of Norouz, the Persian New Year. Norouz begins on the first day of spring and the first day on the Iranian calendar. Norouz has been celebrated for over 3,000 years; it is an integral part of Persian culture. Spring is perfectly celebrated during this holiday. Each day is an affirmation or a renewal in nature and experiencing it helps one enter another plane of existence; it is a feast on the magnificence of living.

I woke up with the singing birds in their leafy cover on the trees by the bedroom window. It was six in the morning. Fortune favored us with a delightful, sunny day. The strong perfume smell of pollinating tuberose coming through the open window was amazing. To my surprise, Ziba was up, dressed, and ready. Sitting on the bed, leaning silently on the pillow, she was ready to go for a discovery. I hadn't heard any noises when she got up. I sat on my bed and I said, "Good morning, Ziba."

She replied, "Good morning."

I said, "You are up very early."

She said, "It is a beautiful morning. I don't want to waste a moment of these blessing times."

As I stretched my arms, looking at her face, I wondered about her thoughts and views of the mountain and the lake in her mind and how those were sounding in her visions. I closed my eyes for a few seconds, imagining no sight. I opened my eyes and I selfishly thought to myself how lucky I was, I had never felt calm so deep!

Smelling the aroma of toasted lavash bread was enticing. It is the Persian tradition that on the first day of the new year everyone wears all new clothes and shoes. I dressed in my new clothes and new shoes, and we went downstairs into the living room where I saw a rustic basket of choice narcissi and hyacinth blooms that could not fail to lift spirits. It was set on the table where the breakfast was ready. Flowers were Mother's trademark.

I love Norouz, especially seeing everyone dressed up. We all gathered around the table. Ali and Akram served the breakfast. I told Ali that I couldn't sleep well last night because his canary was singing all night. He laughed and explained that his canary was blinded by lighting a few months ago in the garden, and it had to be taught to bathe and find its seed and water. Not being able to recognize daylight, now his canary would often start singing at midnight. That made us very sad. We then asked Ali to show us his canary and he said he would.

While eating breakfast, I asked Mother to give Ziba and me permission to walk to the lake by ourselves and spend some time there. At first she was reluctant, but because this was my wish written on the paper, she agreed. We promised not to go far and come back soon.

In my heart I had been kind of scared to go around the lake from the time I had heard from Ali that a young woman had hanged herself there. He had also told us that the bad things had happened there. According to Ali, "The sky began darkening toward the afternoon when villagers found her dead body. Monstrous!" I remember after hearing this story, our faces froze. When Mother asked him, "Why did she hang herself?" Ali answered, "Because she had given birth to a girl instead of boy." After a pause he sighed, "I've heard the husband didn't talk to his wife for weeks, blaming her for not giving him a son who could follow in his footsteps as a shepherd. Akram said that she saw the man irritably crying after the birth of his daughter and he didn't talk to his wife for days. The wife was beaten and hurt by her husband many times. Two month later, his wife, who couldn't bare his abuses, hanged herself on a tree at the lake."

Listening to the story, our faces took on a distressing blankness. We were all almost absurdly sad and scared. I had always been saddened about those women who are living oppressed lives in their husband's homes, dominated by their religious rules.

Ali was always very superstitious. Every time Hassan, his son, was showing too much excitement, yelling and screaming when playing games, Ali would say that he was inhabited by the ghost of that woman who had hanged herself. This suggestion, even as a joke, was frightening to us.

Once I mentioned the ghost story to my father he laughed and said, "Don't you believe Ali; only uneducated people believe in ghosts."

I would be skeptical about the existence of ghost, but in Ali's story, there was something soul-stirring about looking around the lake knowing someone had committed suicide in there.

In spite of all those scary thoughts, as a meditative observer, I tried not to pay attention to it. I was still very excited. We ran upstairs, changed and Mother stopped us in the middle of the porch steps with the shout, "Don't go too far, and come back soon!"

Chapter Seventeen

As we walked back home, I brought up the loss of my best friend who died of leukemia at the age of 8. Her name was Mina. I told Ziba all about my disappointment with God at that time and how I was in a prison of grief and dreary thoughts for a long time after she died. I described her painful death and she became very curious to know what has happened to Mina. A flood of thoughts came over me that filled my eyes with tears as I started to explain:

Mina and I were childhood friends; her parents were our next-door neighbors. We were born the same year and went to school together. She was my best friend. It was exciting to play with her. We used to play tea party with our dolls, climb trees, draw pictures, make up games and play with toys. In the winter, we'd go outside on weekends after breakfast and go sledding or make a snowman, go inside for lunch, and then go out again until dinner. Then we'd sit and play games until bedtime. She was a person who had a knack for quickly grabbing and holding everyone's attention.

Mina became very sick when we were in third grade. We were told by her parents that she had the flu, but Mina had told me secretly that she was sick with a serious disease, leukemia, and her family didn't want anyone to know. When I learned about her illness and that she didn't have much time to live, the stormy winds of anger blew through me.

As time passed, her condition became worse. After summer was over, she came to school every now and then. One day, in the bleak December, the teacher opened the classroom door. No one had any clues as we all cheerfully entered. Suddenly I saw Mina's beautiful picture in the middle of a big bouquet of white flowers hugged with a black and white ribbon. Reading the line of words written on the white ribbon, "Goodbye friends. I have gone to Heaven," I felt as if a needle penetrated my eyes. The flowers rested on her chair with a notepad and a pencil on top of her desk. Surrounded by the chaos of wonder and hearing the voices of heightened dramatic action of the students, our teacher told us to sit and be quiet. Unexpectedly, the room became very quiet as our teacher, Miss Heydari, stood in front of her desk. After a long pause, she gave us the bad news and the "Goodbye, friends" speech as her eyes grew teary. We were seated at our desks when she passed out a funeral flyer. I remember that moment vividly: we all felt a few seconds of shock when we heard our teacher's voice filled with emotion and subdued with regret, tenderness, and pity as she gave us the bad news. With tears in her eyes and a somber tone, she then explained, "As you are aware, Mina was very ill recently. Unfortunately she didn't make it and passed away in the hospital last night."

To our surprise, instead of giving more details about her death, the teacher talked about the omnipotence of spiritual behavior, and spoke to us in a tone of high purpose as she gave us a homogeneous religious speech. Her lecture guaranteed us that Mina is in Heaven now. She then gave a short description of the leukemia symptoms, as if anyone really wanted to know or cared about it at that moment. After reciting the Muslim prayer of mourning, a verse from the holy book of Koran, she then gave us an assignment for the next day. We were to write an essay about Mina and express our feelings about her death. The next day was mainly dedicated to her and each of us had to read our essay in the class. Upon hearing the news, I just sat down and cried silently. That was all I could do. I was unable to accept the truth about her death. I had no recourse but to cry. I recalled how all my little classmates who knew how close friends we had been, came up to my desk, giving me hugs and offering me whatever trinkets they had to comfort me: candy, bubble gum, biscuits.

However, at that moment my faith had started to crack. I thought what convenience were words to fool ourselves about Heaven. Mina's death turned my world of faith upside-down. Mourning her death was about as universal a human emotion as existed. From that day I felt a strange kind of loneliness and I wrestled with the disbelief and couldn't stand the pain. I had a wildfire in the field of my faith. It took me a long while before I was able to get over the loss of my best friend. Nothing felt pleasurable to me. From then on, I was not happy because I hated school. The death of Mina seemed to have been too much to bear. I couldn't study, draw, write poems or even listen to music.

The rest of the time in class, students sat with perfect posture at their desks, while I sat on the edge of my seat; I couldn't wait for the class to be over so I could leave right away. The teacher kept on telling me to sit correctly. My grief matched the intensity of the relationship between Mina and me to the point that my hope was shut very suddenly. Upon hearing the heartbreaking news, I recall, I was in such disbelief that my whole body didn't know how to react. *That is impossible*, I thought to myself, *I just saw her four days ago when I had gone to her house. Outside the front door we talked about her coming back to school and competing again in the spring painting and poetry competition. Her parents had told me the crisis, the danger, had passed; that her lingering illness was over and was conquered at last.* I was confused by all the talks about death.

I had prayed to God every day for her fast recovery, hoping she'd come back to school soon. That night, after hearing the news, I felt a cleaving in my heart as if my heart had split. I sat up all night thinking about Mina. How her loss ended the joy and the hope—all seemed finished! The laughter and the love were gone. The memories, sweet and endless, all came back to me! She died so young and it filled my heart with so much pain and thoughts of flame that shall live within my heart forever. Still as of now, I think no one would ever find the reason for her early death—a great injustice was done. From that day on, I had many dark nights in my soul. My despair only deepened when Mina died. I wrote this poem for her:

> A breath, they say, divides our life and death.
> Now you can see what life depends upon...
> A blessing; we should use it, as life goes on.
> For it is fated to live just one time!

Ziba had said, "What a beautiful poem."
I sighed. "That was the last poem I wrote until I met you."
She smiled and said, "What did you write in your essay about Mina?"
The next day, I recalled, I was so depressed I could hardly get out of bed. I didn't want to go to school, but my father forced me to go. In class, sitting in my chair, as I was listening to the students' essays, I couldn't help but gaze at Mina's empty seat. My faith in God was wrecked, and a terrible storm suddenly passed over me. The pen fell powerless from my shaking hand and tears poured from my eyes. I couldn't write. I couldn't speak. I couldn't feel or think. Standing motionless and grieving, my heart was saddened and restless, and my thoughts were full of questions for God: *Why did she die so soon? Why, God? Why?*

In class, listening to each essay, the burden laying upon my mind seemed much greater than I could understand or bear. I asked teacher to be excused, and she gave me permission to leave the classroom. Dropping my paper, I left angrily and created a misshapen chaos among the student. Ten minutes later, I was returned by the Principal to class. I sat at my desk, filled with anger. It was my turn to read my essay. I stood up in front of the students, and with fierce tears, I breathlessly read my short essay with all my might: "To my best friend Mina, who was taken from us unfairly while God watched and did nothing. I don't know why or where you were taken or whether I may ever see you again. Goodbye, my friend, and good luck finding a Heaven up there!"

All eyes were focused on me, which, of course, was something I had hoped to avoid, along with being there in the first place. My farewell essay and poem had shocked everyone.

Standing there, watching all of them staring at me, some in shock, some in anger, a few looked confused, half in doubt and half in wonder, as if they were guessing my faith, but expressing no words. The teacher seemed sorry for me, but simultaneously disappointed, she irritably told me to sit down at my seat.

At recess, Mrs. Heydari said, "You're all excused to go out and play, except Azadeh." She then called me to her desk and said, "You will stay inside and read the Koran from page 1 to 10."

I preferred to do arithmetic problems; I felt that would be a lighter punishment. In those days, no one could express any doubts or anger about God and teachers took care of minor infractions and discipline problems. This was fortunate for me because if she had told the principal or our religion instructor about my essay, I could have been in greater trouble and risked expulsion from school as an atheist.

The rest of the year was an eternity, yet what volumes may be drawn from my paintings with little drops of ink or paint! In the lonely hours, at silent morning or at midnight, my eyes filled with tears; the doubts, the anger, the unknown callous pains had inflicted my body with a fever that hurt my brain with the burning words: *Why did she die? Why, God? Why?*

A picture of Mina would come and went in my mind. I remember how often, in the days that had gone by, I gazed at her empty chair in the classroom and had illusions, recalling how in her brief existence she was so eager to participate in every art class and win the art competitions. Every day I yearned for Mina, looking for her in a crowd of students in our class, or expecting her to call or to come to my home. I didn't have ordinary grief; I had a persistent grief in my brain. I had wished that God didn't take her so soon.

Ziba and I spent a lot of time in the garden, discussing in great depth religion, life, poetry and art. I spent a lot of time describing to Ziba the sights of the garden, the pine forests, the hummingbirds, the deeply green grass, the color of the wild flowers, the happy birds building nests in the tree and the raspberries growing precariously by the brook. We picked bouquets of wildflowers so fragrant, their perfume nearly overpowered us.

We took our time getting back to the house from the lake, just laughing, talking and reveling in our freedom. Ziba told me she was glad we invited her on the trip, that it was the first New Year she had truly enjoyed.

I exclaimed, "Let's have some fun. We'll run as fast as we can!" We started running around, frolicking and dancing the dance only a carefree child can.

We spent luxurious minutes frantically running in the spring sun, our faces purplish red and sweaty, with still half a mile to go before reaching the house. We smiled cheerfully, hand in hand, with a handful of great, big wildflowers clutched in our free hand. We sang into the breeze and plopped down into a tuft of wavy grass to catch our breath underneath a blossoming peach tree. As I drew in deep gulps of fresh air and leaned down to pick another flower, Ziba said something I couldn't quite catch.

I felt a sharp pain in my right leg and screamed loudly, feeling a rush of panic flood my body; I had been bitten by a snake. I had no idea how Ziba could find me help. I felt a burning sensation in my leg.

"Oh my God!" Ziba yelled over and over again. "Oh God!"

"Stop calling God as if God exists," I chided her in a trembling voice. "Don't stand there! Run and get help."

My heart was pounding fast and I shook in a mixture of fear and pain. Ziba wanted to try to walk home, but I was completely torn apart and steadfastly refused.

"I can't walk any farther!" I cried. "My leg is too sore and if I try to move or run, snake poison could speed up in my blood and I could die. Just go and find someone to help me!"

She paused for an excruciating second, and then assured me God was with me and she'd be back with help as soon as possible. I just turned her body toward the house and told her to run straight and she did. As I followed her with my eyes, she took off in an erratic run.

"Faster, faster!" I chanted.

I finally gathered up the courage to look at my leg. With hands shaking in fear, I looked around for something to splint the ankle, realizing after a few seconds that I couldn't reach the area to try to suck the poison out. I just sat there, motionless, thinking the affected limb should be moved as little as possible to delay absorption of the venom. I didn't move.

Now frozen with fear, I took a deep breath and lay on the ground, closed my eyes and waited for the end to come. I was scared, panicked, fatigued and very numb from the right knee down. I recalled Ziba's constant words that faith in God helps you climb out of your fear. With my heart thumping in my chest, certain I was going to die, I thought maybe I could be a friend with God. For the first time in my life I appealed to God to save me. Suddenly, a flood of remorse and an overwhelming sense of submission rushed into my head. I fell upon my knees, not feeling any pain, and started reciting any holy prayer I could think of in sheer panic, in hopes of being forgiven by God so He would save my life.

"Oh, good God. I am sorry I doubted you; I don't know why I couldn't believe before that you are up there, but now I just do! Please help me. Please don't let me die here," I said over and over. "If you save me, I'll believe in your existence." My heartbeat and breathing became faster. I didn't see anyone approaching, just beautiful butterflies waltzing around my head.

I suddenly heard my mother and father coming. I sat up and saw them running toward me. I breathed a sigh of relief. "Are you all right?" Father asked worriedly.

"I guess, but I feel a lot of pain in my leg," I said tearfully. "Mother, is Ziba alright?"

Mother, who was in tears and panic, said, "Yes, yes, she's fine."

Father wanted to know where the snake bite was. As I looked up into his face, too horrified to move, I showed him my leg. Father calmly took charge and tended to me and said, "It is not a big deal. It is just a bite, but we should take you to the doctor just in case."

Kneeling down behind me, picking me up under my arms, he effortlessly carried me to his car. He drove toward a small clinic in the village while Mother sat silently in the front seat next to him, glancing back at me now and then to see if I was fine. After a short drive, we arrived at the clinic. The doctor wasn't in, but a nurse inspected the wound, looking for broken teeth or a second bite. She cleaned it with large amount of soap and water, and then gave me two shots in my arms: Tetanus and antivenom. All I could hear was the blood pounding in my ears. She gave Father a few antibiotics for me that would prevent infection.

Driving back home, I lay down in the back seat of the car and thought how my mother had a special way of making every person in any emergency feel calm, loved and not to be blamed; how she would overlook little faults to find the good things. I also thought of Ziba and how she never failed as my friend. As soon as we reached home, everybody greeted me as if I was returning from a battleground. When I saw Ziba, I was shocked. Her upper lip was swollen and red. She looked very funny!

"What happened to your lip? Did you fall down?" I asked.

She smiled and said, "No, when I was running to get help I was stung by a bee."

I was overwhelmed with guilt. "Does it hurt?"

"Compared to your snake bite, not at all," she said and smiled.

Chapter Eighteen

I rested in bed all afternoon. Ziba and I couldn't stop talking about the drama of the morning: my snake bite, my near death experience and Ziba's courage. We laughed at my reaction after the snake bite and how frantically she ran toward some unknown destination to find my mother. It seemed very funny now and we laughed so hard we couldn't breathe.

I described the snakebite as an accident, bad luck even, but she described it as God helping me to survive. I didn't argue with her. I couldn't believe that the power of the mind had so far remained unnoticed in my world. After being bitten by the snake, I had for a short time discovered God and how His word could deceive fear. As I lay on the ground, convinced God was watching over me, I had felt my helplessness feather away. I had felt calm.

Ziba wanted to know if I now believed in God. I paused before answering yes. She was elated until I added, "I'm fine with religion and God, and I can understand that faith plays a role in the power of the mind."

She chuckled and said, "Even if you believe in God for just a short time, He is like a balm for your soul."

"Don't push it. I still need stronger evidence," I laughed.

A few nights when everyone else was asleep, Ziba and I would sneak out of bed, grab a star chart and peer at the night sky through the patio door. I looked at the night sky and described what I saw for Ziba. I stole a glance at Ziba to see how she reacted to my description; to my amazement, she was looking at the sky totally transfixed. I let her imagination roam free.

One night, after supper, I dragged everyone outside with flashlights in hand. We all gathered in the dark at the center of the garden and despite the mosquitoes, gazed at the sky that was heavy with stars. Sometimes the moon seemed so close that I wanted to raise my hands and touch it.

Spending so many hours with Ziba on this trip had permanently enriched my life. She couldn't see a thing but she had a sense of playfulness that made my childhood magical. While helping Ziba pack her clothes for the trip back home, I told her that this trip felt like the birthday of my new life that has brought forth new blossoms of art in me. I don't know why, but somehow, I had received from her a charge to find God in my heart. She told me how much she enjoyed the trip and more than anything else, enjoyed taking hot showers instead of the bucket showers she took at home.

One of the things we did some mornings was to go on top of the small hill by the lake where my brothers and Hassan had brought some huge, truck inner tubes. It was fun to watch them rolling downhill in the tube. This small town was like heaven to us. It was blessed with three fine places to picnic, and all were packed with families during the New Year holiday. I always thought that when I had my own family I would try to carry on the picnic tradition. One day when we all went to shop in the village, we saw a man simultaneously singing, dancing and playing the Dayereh-Zangi, the Persian tambourine. These were New Year shows, mostly with men performing in blackface and, in their delight, they would get people to cheer and laugh at them for money. They were called "Haji-Firooz." This is the only tradition of Norouz that I never liked because I always thought it was racist.

We had a long vacation in the mountains and came home with a lifetime's worth of happy memories. It seemed Ziba had the best time too, because she kept thanking us. As Father was driving through the village, Mother remarked how quickly the time had passed, and in a way it was true. What a glorious time we had! Ziba said that she never felt like this. Father laughed and said, "Yes, this is a heavenly place. Except for one rather nasty day, we've had a blissful time."

Three days after the trip, Ziba came to our house, and she had taped twenty minutes of new poems that were all about our New Year trip. Even after spending so much time with her, I was amazed to hear her vivid descriptions that she wrote about beauties she'd never actually seen.

She told me several times during our vacation that though she was blind and could not see the world like the rest of us, she was going to be a poet. She wanted to write poetry with enthusiasm, zeal and the same passion she put into being a good person.

I learned from Ziba how a spiritual approach to life can bring together the desperate areas of our human experience; how it can be emotional as well as intellectual. Gradually, I realized how God's word has a magic power on my actions and gives me energy when I need to face life's turbulence.

Chapter Nineteen

Ziba's mother, in a perilous financial state, married Rahmat when Ziba was 16. Rahmat already had four children from his other wife. He called them "hey you," and he called Ziba "the blind one." This was the time Ziba's life truly fell into despair. She, however, kept up her positive outlook. I found it easy to be swept up in her enthusiasm but it broke my heart to hear her gentle voice making plans that would likely never happen.

I feverishly prayed to God to help her, especially after the family moved into to a house where all eight slept in a single room under a leaky thatch roof. For the next six years, she lived a turbulent life, a real hell. She'd been beaten, berated and starved. She weighed maybe 90 pounds. Money was short, but my family had persuaded Sima to resist the temptation to send Ziba to an orphanage. Her melancholy was an intensifying element in much of Ziba's verses. Occasionally anger flared up in her poems, but in recent years I had noted the suffering becoming more and more apparent in her verses. There was no solution in sight for her. In poor health due to a lack of nourishment, Ziba just kept willing herself to live. Two years later, Rahmat moved them to an enclosed house that had neither electricity nor clean water and was shared by the extended family. The small toilet located at the far corner of the house served 15 people. Rahmat wouldn't allow her outside. She was responsible for cleaning the house and weaving scarves and socks for the family.

I became increasingly angry over the years, mainly from Ziba's justification for Rahmat's hideous deeds. I often wondered how she could remain so positive. She composed the poems so delicately about the hurt.

As time passed, we couldn't spend as much time together as we once did. Ziba continued to look thin, pale and neglected. A year before I left Iran, she confided that she felt the unhappiness in her life was too much. I realized how her optimism was being tempered by memories from the past. Frustrations over her mother's marriage, rising tides of verbal and physical abuses, moving from one place to another—she felt it was all getting too difficult.

She had to hide her poetry tapes from Rahmat. One day he found the tape recorder under her pillow. After he smashed it, he tossed the tapes out the window and screamed in her face and shoved her against the wall and told her, "Stop writing poetry. You are infecting your brain. Enough is enough!" He then told her that she should have been reciting verses from the holy book of Koran instead of composing her blasphemous desires on tape. He gave her two weeks to memorize the entire Koran. She already knew most of the holy book by heart but by the end of the two weeks, not only had she memorized the Koran, but she could also recite some of the major verses backwards!

The last year of high school was the busiest year for me. Not only did I have to study for finals, I also had to study for the university entrance exams. The entrance exams were held only once a year for admission into all the universities in Iran. Ziba and I couldn't spend much time together, but when we did, we would talk for hours.

My heart broke to hear Ziba finally admit she had been defeated by life. Ziba's spiritual poems were growing darker and every time I told her that I had seen how the turbulences in her life had evoked a shift in her composing, she'd say that she did not even realize her mind was becoming negative.

A few months before I left Iran, Rahmat's abuses were exacerbated and for the first time I heard Ziba say surviving was difficult. She slumped into a deep melancholy.

I tried to give her hope, but she was really struggling to reinforce her own optimism. Rahmat had beaten and manipulated it out of her. He schemed to keep her away from our home.

The day I left Iran, I felt as if I had left a huge part of me behind. It was one of the saddest days in my life.

Chapter Twenty

Four months after I left Iran, I heard from my father that Ziba and her mother had died. They passed away on November 20, 1976 on brutally cold day in Tabriz. Ziba was 24. They died in their sleep, suffocated by carbon monoxide that seeped out of a faulty heater in their room.

I will never forget the shock of the news. It was so difficult to bear, and even harder to believe. After hearing the news from my father in Iran, I stood there, motionless for a moment, my heart lurching and my legs wanting to quit me. I felt my world rock on its foundation.

There are moments in life when you just feel powerless. For me, this was one of those times. I was so sad that I wanted to retreat to a faraway corner of the world, where all the cacophony and distress couldn't find me. My life came to a virtual standstill. I spent hours on my bed weeping tears of sadness and pain. I couldn't believe that she was dead and gone. I had given her my tape recorder before I left and she sent me the poems right before she died. They were full of raunchy complaint, self-deprecating humor, and descriptions of her suffering; all her hopes and dreams had been violently snuffed out. I hesitated to transcribe her poems because I couldn't bear to see wave after wave of disappointment.

It was not clear how Ziba and Sima died, but there was a troubling rumor that they had committed suicide. I asked Mother if she believed Ziba had ended her own life. Her answer was an unequivocal 'no.' Even in pain, even with no hope of it ever getting better, Ziba's religious beliefs would not have allowed her to commit suicide. It remained uncertain if their deaths were by suicide from carbon monoxide poisoning, but I got a pretty clear notion of what could have happened as she hinted at her feelings the day I left Iran: that her own days were waning and that she was exhausted from the ceaseless physical and psychological pain of living with a beast. She had felt the breezes from the afterlife cross her face.

After Ziba's death, my artistic inspiration dried up for a few weeks until my mother brought me files from Iran that contained a number of Ziba's recent verses. They all reflected the intensity of her spiritual emotions. I frequently wept and had flashbacks as I read her poems that were mainly spiritual, creative work that were reflections on pain and hope, love and friendship, prophecy and the miracles of living. But in her passing she reminded me of what matters most. Every time I am down, her cherished voice would ring out in my mind, bringing positivity inside me to comfort my soul. Remembering good things every day, I thank God for people like her in life. As days come and go, often in my lonely hours I have thought of Ziba, who taught me both the richness and limitations of living life.

When I finally finished telling Nina the life story of Ziba, her eyes welled up with tears. She was saddened yet amazed by Ziba's positivity in the face of debilitating diversity.

"What a tragedy!" Nina sniffled. "I'd really be interested to read some of her poetry."

"They were never published," I said, wiping tears from my own eyes. "But I always share her passion for living with my friends." I recited one of Ziba's last poems for Nina:

WITHOUT YOU
Oh God,
Without you, who am I?
A leaf lost in a river,
Soaking for the hope of living forever?
Without you, who am I?
A half-hearted woman,
Searching for your love
To combine with mine?
Without you, who am I?
A homeless wanderer?
Where shall I go
If not to you?
Without you, who am I?
A short sentence with no point
No meaning—nothing?
Wheels turn,
So does life.
I must move on with you…

"Although I had always struggled with spirituality outside the dramas of life, I now know how religion is a necessary condition for some people's happiness," I stated.

"I agree," Nina said, "for some, spirituality is the only means of doing, feeling and responding to life."

Chapter Twenty-One

Many years went by and Nina and I would meet most days, sometimes in her gallery or at one of our homes for tea or lunch. A few months after my daughter was born, Nina invited me to lunch at her house. I had just finished a painting, using the techniques she had taught me. I asked her to appraise my painting, and as always, without any hesitation, she agreed to do it. Nina had a sound knowledge of many painting techniques and her invaluable advice and moral support helped me to improve my work. She always responded enthusiastically to my requests, especially when it was about painting or poetry. It was very important and exciting to hear her opinion each time I finished a new painting. I found her an honest critic who offered constructive criticism.

Although Nina was a perfectionist, her criticism was always sufficiently strong that it laid the groundwork for me to challenge my ability by trying new writing and painting styles. I came to highly value her grasp of art judgment. I hated the idea that some people would feel pressured to give me a lot of phony admiration about my paintings. I brought this up with her during our talks and she laughed and said that people are just trying to be kind.

When I arrived at her house, she showed me such generous hospitality. She was always very elegant in how she set the table and served food and she was a great cook. We had tea and talked about my daughter. I told her how she kept me very busy all the time, but how much she had filled my life with joy. Nina was regretful that she couldn't have any children and had never adopted. After talking for awhile, she decided to write the painting description for the appraisal. Shortly after she began writing, the telephone rang. She excused herself and went to the room in the back of the hall. I heard her talking to someone on the phone in a conversation that was full of emotion and urgency.

After almost ten minutes talking on the phone, she returned into the living room looking very nervous and upset. She apologized and told me the call was from her sister. "My sister told me that she is ill. She wasn't feeling good and wanted me to go to her house and stay with her for awhile," Nina explained. Nina's car was in the repair shop so I said, "I can take you there."

To my surprise, she said, "No, thanks. She'll be alright. Golda is not really sick. She is just depressed." She sat down in her chair and offered me a piece of cake. While we were eating, the telephone rang again.

After going to the same room and talking for less than a minute, she returned to the living room and said, "It was Golda again!"

I expressed my concern and said, "Are you sure you don't want to go? I can take you there."

Nina said, "Oh, no, believe me that it's not really necessary. Her situation is not an emergency; she is just depressed as usual." Nina looked anguished as she continued with her explanation. "Often I ask her, 'How much pain do you want to inflict on you and me?'"

"Why do you think Golda can't overcome her depression?" I asked.

"Because she brings it on herself! You know, I hate to spend time with my sister. Sometimes I think she is no different than a stone, a piece of wood, or something rotten. She stares at the television day and night. Like today, she was nagging on the phone. I told her to go outside and take in some fresh air; to take some deep breaths. I am intolerant of her crude manners and disregard for happiness. Adaptation is the most striking fact about life and Golda's lack of adaptation is the reason for her unsuccessful life, or at least for a fighting chance."

As we were talking, the phone rang again. She went into the same room and shortly after she returned and told me, "This time I didn't even answer it. I took the phone off the hook because I am sure it was Golda again."

I told Nina I wanted to meet Golda, "Why don't I take you two to lunch next week? My treat."

"I think she needs more time to get over her attitude and depression," Nina replied. "But that is a good idea, I'll arrange something soon."

As she started to take measurements of my painting, I asked her about the pictures that were sitting on top of the glass table at the far end of the living room.

"Are these pictures of your relatives?" I asked.

"No," she said, "those are the pictures of my husband's relatives, my friends and great aunt and uncles."

"Do you have any pictures of Golda here?" Somehow I had become so curious that I couldn't wait to see Golda, even in a picture.

"I do not have any pictures of her in this room. Most of my immediate family's pictures are upstairs in my bedroom."

I stood up and went to see the pictures. As I was looking at each picture, I noticed a tall, gorgeous woman standing next to Nina. "Who is this beautiful woman in this picture?" I asked.

"That is my best friend Olga."

"She looks like a movie star."

She sighed, "She was more beautiful in person. She was a famous model." Then, unexpectedly, she blurted, "Olga died so unpardonably young."

"How did she die?" I asked quietly.

At this point, Nina stood up, walked toward me and picked up one of those pictures, and said, "Do you want to hear her story?"

"Yes," I answered, "of course."

We often shared memories of our friends; especially our childhood friends but talking about this particular friend brought her to tears when she began telling me Olga's story.

Chapter Twenty-Two

"The first time I met Olga was in September 1930, in high school," Nina started, "I was a new student at our high school then.

"On that day, after history class, Olga walked up to me in the hallway. After introducing herself, she immediately asked me if I was from Poland. 'Yes!' I exclaimed, 'But how do you know?'

"'I guessed from your name,' she replied, 'and you look Polish.'

"After a short conversation about our families, she surprisingly invited me to lunch at her house that same weekend. From that day, until the day she died, we became close friends. Our common thoughts, opinions, memories and feelings about life made it easy for us to identify with each other and I knew from the start that we would be lifelong friends. Olga was one of my best friends; she was without a doubt the most enthusiastic and trustful woman I have ever known. One of Olga's most salient qualities was honesty, often to the point of doing herself a disservice.

"Olga was very beautiful: she was tall and slender with bright blue eyes and long blond hair. She had won a reputation for both her beauty and her impervious personality. She could speak excellent French which she had learned early on from her mother. Olga was born to a Polish father who had immigrated to California from Poland to establish an American branch of his family's wine business. Her mother was French and her family had been successful perfume merchants.

"The summer after high school graduation, we went to the Yosemite National Park. That was the best trip we had together. She was a very fun person to be around and we kept one another laughing the whole time we were there. The only thing I didn't like about Olga was her extreme fascination with butterflies and her collection of them. On that trip I'd taken my kite; as I flew it in the park I found myself lifted into the air by my kite. I always felt that the kite lifted more than just my spirit; it lifted my worries to the sky. Olga would come armed with nets and poison jars to capture butterflies and pin them in glass cases. I hated that. I told her that we should only be charmed with a butterfly's captivating colors and the graceful dance of their mesmerizing wings and never stop them from flying. She laughed and jokingly told me that I don't sense the pleasure of collecting beauties in a glass case; that art is not only captured on a canvas.

"Olga had a dream to become a model. After graduating from high school, she went to modeling school and over the next several years her career blossomed. As time passed, she became very successful in her modeling career and was recognized everywhere. She was, inevitably, the center of attention. Most men around her were magnetically attracted to her, like moths to a flame. You can't imagine the unbelievable number of men that had been interested in marrying her!" Nina exclaimed reflectively.

"She always told me that her beauty wouldn't last long," Nina continued, "so she invested most of her money into real estate where she then made a fortune and became a very wealthy woman. She had soon maintained a steady income stream well beyond her working years.

"In the height of Olga's fame and career, she met a handsome young man. His name was Albert. He was smart, funny, and charming. He had a reputation of being able do numbers in his head quicker than a calculator. In the company where he was working he had a strong reputation of being a wheeler-dealer businessman and a great bargainer.

"Olga wasn't particularly interested in getting married or having children, but, somehow, Albert convinced her to marry him. Albert was the soul mate Olga had been searching for. As an investment counselor he not only gained her trust but she soon fell feverishly in love with him. I remember the first time I met Albert. I didn't like him because I noted in every conversation we had, he talked about money and investment as if these were the roots of happiness. Gradually, I recognized that he wanted to be liked and approved of by everyone and he measured his value by the attention he got from others. In turn, he valued others by measuring how much money or assets they had. I had problems with him, but I kept them buried deep in my gut.

"Olga and Albert dated for a short time and the following year, in the summer of 1942, they got married. They settled in Olga's mansion in Beverly Hills, with a second home in Malibu so they could be close to the ocean. Olga enjoyed considerable success and happiness in the first years of their marriage. In the second year, she became pregnant with their first child and her daughter was born in 1944. The thing struck me the most about Olga was right after the birth of her first child, not only had she stopped collecting butterflies, but she donated all her beloved collections to the Museum of Science in Los Angeles. On the day her daughter was born I went to visit Olga in the hospital; she cried and told me that, now, being a mother, she was ashamed of capturing all those butterflies.

"Two years later, their second daughter was born. It seemed they had a happy marriage; everything was going smoothly until the day when it all fell apart: Olga was convinced that Albert was having an affair with their servant, Anna. Olga didn't confront Albert about the affair, instead, she fired Anna!" Nina exclaimed while shaking her head in disgust. "More trouble started brewing when Olga started suspecting Albert of committing more adultery; he had begun having an affair with his secretary. Olga enlisted the services of a private investigator and, in one year, Albert had had affairs with two women and had been secretly spending time with them in their Malibu house.

"Olga's idyllic way of life abruptly ended when she found out about her husband's extramarital affairs. Many times she talked to me about her plans to put an end to their relationship, but she still had a lot of mixed feelings about divorce. The last time we talked about discussing her options she told me, 'Although it is very hurtful and uncomfortable for me, I've decided to ignore Albert's cheating; I want to wait until my daughters are grown up, past their teenage years, then I'll file for divorce.'

"The idea was that her daughters would have a better understanding of the reasons for their parents' divorce when they were adults. She intended to be a good and dedicated mother to her children by not dragging them in to her own life conflicts with their father. I strongly disagreed with her plan and advised her against it; I forcibly argued with Olga to get a divorce. I told her that she is sweeping the dust of her problems under the rug and ignorance is not a good solution; a lack of accountability and consequence only fuels moral corruption.

"Matters became more complicated when a writer from a New York magazine was sent to her house to interview Olga. The writer, Sydney, was supposed to write an article about Olga's life and family. Apparently, Albert had met the glamorous journalist and after the interview, he offered her ride to her hotel. The love affair between Sydney and Albert was inevitable. Shortly after, Albert stopped seeing other women and in December of 1952, the private detective Olga had hired proved, again, that Olga's fear had materialized: he took pictures showing the reclusive Albert with Sydney. The pair was photographed at their Malibu house, the Beverly Hills hotel and multiple restaurants. Sydney, apparently, had moved from New York to Hollywood. In secret, she continued to spend more time with Albert. They had fallen wildly in love with each other. Olga learned from the investigator that Albert had met with an attorney and was planning to file for divorce.

"As this painful life and saga was going on, tragedy struck: Olga got a terrifying diagnosis of late-stage ovarian cancer at the age of 36. At the beginning she was upbeat as usual until the second news brought even more devastation: she learned that she had only a few months to live.

"At first, Albert seemed like he had great sympathy for Olga and he stopped seeing Sydney for a while. But, within a few weeks, he renewed his relationship with her. Olga lost all hope and her unhappiness over Albert's unfaithfulness was aggravated by quarrels over money and his spending. Albert had spent tens of thousands of dollars to fund his own interests without telling Olga, who had been in and out of the hospital.

"According to Olga, she learned about the missing funds only when her long term accountant came forward, saying he could no longer continue to dole out cash to Albert. At one point, her investigator had even heard Albert saying to Sydney that the end is near and he wanted to stay with Olga until the last day so he can inherent all her wealth.

"Olga had a cheating husband, a dying body, no hope and no future and one night, in March 1953, she developed a terrible fever. The medicines she was given were not working and as the days wore on, she developed an infection and her fever grew worse.

"A night before she died, Olga called me around 12 midnight. I knew it must have been something very important, because she had never called me that late before. I picked up the phone and hearing her sad voice on the line, she gave me the bad news. She said that in the afternoon she felt extremely sick and the team of doctors she had hurriedly consulted admitted there was little hope. My heart started to pound as I listened to her: 'The doctors told me that I have 24 hours to live!' She then asked me to be in her house at seven o'clock in the morning. Horribly sad and with tears falling from my eyes, I said, 'Of course, I'll be there.' She mentioned that her immediate family members, with the exception of her daughters, would be there too. She said, 'I want to have a little fun with my family before I leave this world.'

"'What do you mean?' I asked her.

"'You'll see,' she replied, 'just be here on time.'

"'I will,' I promised and we said goodbye and hung up the phone."

Chapter Twenty-Three

"On the day Olga died," Nina continued, "I arrived at her house early in the morning. I rang the doorbell and heard the footsteps of her old maid and longtime confidant. The door opened and I saw tears in the eyes of the long-boned, large-eyed woman.

"She gave me a short hug and said, 'Olga is terribly excited about seeing you! Everyone is here and awaiting for you upstairs.' She urged me to hurry upstairs. 'There's not much time left,' she said worriedly. Her wrinkled face streamed with tears and before I could say anything to comfort her, she quickly said, 'Hurry, there's not much time to lose. Go!'

"Running upstairs, I headed for Olga's big bedroom. Just a few steps from her room, I stopped. I took a deep breath and stood there for a few seconds, trying to muster my flagging courage. I wasn't sure I could bear to see my best friend on her death bed.

"'Regardless of how this turns out, I should try to stay calm,' I told myself, saying a short prayer for comfort. I opened the bedroom door while my body continued to shake like an earthquake.

"Inside the bedroom, Olga lay in her big bed. She was pale faced and bald; she hadn't covered her head in the colorful scarf she normally wore. Seeing her in that condition, there was no longer any doubt in my mind that her life was about to end at any moment. Family members were sprawled across the bed. Her husband Albert sat down beside her on the bed. With the exception of two people-a gray haired man who stood at the desk and a beautiful young woman who was seated on a chair close to the window-I knew everyone there. I guessed the man to be Olga's attorney and the woman must have been Sydney. As I walked in, I headed directly over to Olga's bed. When I saw her up close, it was clear that nothing could save her, but lying in the bed she was calm as ever and the room was just as quiet as if no one was in there. Olga looked as if she had been given a lot of morphine. It was clear her end was near.

"There were at least ten people in the room; the lead actors in a dynastic drama that will determine just who would be an heir to the multi-million dollar fortune that Olga had barely touched in her lifetime.

"I gently took her hand and smiled. I kissed both her cheeks and after a long hug, a troubled silence fell between us until she cheekily whispered to me, 'I'm so glad you're here. It's my last show, you know.'

"I sat down in a nearby chair and assessed everybody. My attention had sharpened at Olga's words, and I started thinking she might have prepared something in her will to embarrass Albert and Sydney in front of everybody there. At first, I found myself at odds to be sitting among all of them and next to Sydney. Without looking at each other, we just sat there. All my attention was now toward Olga. *I shall miss her terribly*. I thought to myself.

"Albert was crying softly in steady little sobs while wiping his tears every few seconds. I felt an unexpected flash of sympathy for him even though I knew his tears were pretend and not of passion.

"A short silence was broken by Olga sitting up and asking her attorney, Mr. Fitzgerald, to start reading her will.

"Olga, with a low, weak voice, said, 'I love you all, thank you for coming here today. This is my last wish, to be with all of my favorite people in this world.' She then motioned toward me and said, 'I am especially grateful to two friends for being here today: Nina, who asked me on the telephone last night what I wished to do today. I told her I'd rather not die, but of course, that is not my choice. So I told her, reading my will is my last wish.'

"Looking at Olga" Nina continued, "I felt she was torn between longing to die and clinging to life. I had detected in her a quite strong desire to live after she found out about her cancer. To my surprise, at this time she introduced Sydney by motioning toward her with a bittersweet smile, as if remembering a tumultuous marriage.

"'I also thank Miss Sydney, who is a great news writer; she was kind enough to join us today to interview me for the last time.' She then took a deep breath and exhaled with a bitter smile on her face and continued, 'Hopefully Sydney will write about me even after I leave this world.'

"Looking at Sydney, a charming woman indeed with a slender, pretty face, I struggled not to roll my eyes. Olga spoke so calmly, so pleasantly, that I got the idea that in her heart she had forgiven Sydney and Albert. I thought to myself, *this reporter is no lady, but a hot slut*. I had the impression that the dying woman lying in front of her didn't mean anything to her.

"I wasn't sure what I should be expecting from Olga's will, but suddenly I was excited. The moments of putting out the fire of curiosity arrived when

Mr. Fitzgerald started to read it. As he began reading the will, I noticed Albert's eyes narrow and glimmer. Shortly, his face turned red and tears began to pour out of his eyes. It was all he could do to keep his hands at his side. Finally, he put his arm around Olga, looking ridiculously nervous the whole time.

"'Why does she want to do this?' I asked myself, puzzled. I guessed that she wanted to see the expression on her family member's faces when they learned what they would inherit from her. I was really moved when I heard the contents of the will. Albert was left in charge of her estate, plus he would be given a check for the sale of hundreds of pieces of her jewelry, as well as important works of art, including paintings by Rembrandt, Rubens and Picasso. But, the amount of the check wouldn't be disclosed to him until after Olga's burial. She left everything else in trust to her children with Albert as the executor. In addition to all of that, Olga also gave smaller bequests to a few other people and her favorite charities. I too, was given a few paintings that I had always loved, as well as two very expensive statues and a two month paid trip to Poland.

"Olga looked pensive, but looking at Albert's expression suggested a huge satisfaction, rather than shame. At first, I thought he was the man who had never stopped cheating and was counting how many days she had left to live. I had assumed she was going to launch a surprise attack by disinheriting him from her wealth, yet she wrote a check for Albert. I couldn't help thinking how it was the strangest mixture of generosity and forgiveness. In my heart, I wished my sister could have been like Olga: kind and full of forgiveness. I was so thankful that her life was ending with forgiveness for Albert, even though he did not deserve it."

Chapter Twenty-Four

"Two days after Olga's funeral, I was still in bed," Nina continued. "On the third day, I got a call from Mr. Fitzgerald out of the blue asking me to meet with him in his office the next day. He said he had important news for Albert and I was to be there. As curious as I was, I didn't want to go, but Mr. Fitzgerald insisted. He called it an urgent matter and said Olga had wanted me to be there when Albert was presented a check from the sale of Olga's things. All night, I thought about Olga and the memories from her happier days-her wedding to Albert, the birth of her beautiful daughters-flashed through my mind.

"The next day I was so weak that I had to call a taxi to take me to Mr. Fitzgerald's office. I arrived there almost thirty minutes early. Mr. Fitzgerald finished up a meeting with another client and called me into his office.

"I sat down on the chair in front of his desk. I saw a few pictures of him with famous people and movie stars on a long mahogany table behind his desk. He was one of the most powerful and reputable attorneys in Beverly Hills. He was also Olga's chief confidant who had known her since her childhood. After a short while the door opened and there was Albert, arm-in-arm with Sydney! The only thing that came to my mind at that moment was how shameless this man was. They entered into the room where we both shook hands with them. Needless to say, they were so shocked to see me there, that for a few seconds, Albert wasn't sure what to say. I, too, was very uncomfortable being in his presence.

"Sydney wore a tailored black suit and black fishnet stockings. She bore a tentative yet steely smile. There was a polite and uneasy silence as I sneaked a glance at Albert, who was watching Mr. Fitzgerald rifle through papers on his desk. Albert gave me a curious glance.

"Mr. Fitzgerald cleared his throat. 'The reason I asked you here today is because Olga made a few changes in her will before she passed away,' he said slowly and methodically.

"'What?' Albert bellowed in shock, 'What do you mean, 'changes'?'

"Mr. Fitzgerald explained, 'Olga asked me to prepare two wills for her. The first was the one I read in Olga's presence. She signed this one just before she passed away. On that day, when she asked you all to leave her room, it was because she wanted to sign her last will.'

"According to the new will, Albert was just entitled to a check written personally by Olga. Mr. Fitzgerald handed Albert an envelope and told Albert he could cash the check inside at anytime.

"Albert's smile was clipped and I watched in fascination, wondering how much the check was for, how Albert would react and what Olga had had in mind.

"'What about the new will? What has been changed in it?' Albert asked.

"Mr. Fitzgerald handed me a big yellow envelope and asked me to open it and read the final will out loud to all. In the chaos of confusion and curiosity, I just followed his instruction. Opening the envelope, I pulled out the will and started to read. It was in that moment that we all learned that Olga had revised many terms in her will; she had done the unthinkable! According to Mr. Fitzgerald, a few months before she died, Olga sold all her expensive jewelry, her collectables, and her paintings for one million dollars; a far higher price than anyone could have predicted. In her final will, Olga left everything to her children and appointed me and Mr. Fitzgerald as the executors of her estate. When I finished reading the will, Albert opened his envelope, clearly hoping the check inside would be for a substantial amount. His eyes bulged when he looked at the check. He looked furious.

"At that moment, I realized he must not have gotten the amount he hoped for. Olga had left him just $1.

"'Olga sold her business to protect her children from you,' Mr. Fitzgerald said. 'She thought you would run her wealth into the ground if she left everything to you.'

"'No! This can not be true!' Albert frantically replied. 'A check for a dollar? There must have been some big mistake! Are you playing a game with me?'

"'This is what I was instructed by Olga to do. There's been no mistake,' Mr. Fitzgerald said.

"*Hooray!* I thought to myself. *What retribution! This is what Albert deserves for cheating all those years.*

"Albert believed he was entitled to more of the estate and demanded a copy of the will and trust. He made objection after objection and said he could prove that she was incompetent when the will was signed; that she was mentally unstable and confused from painkillers before her death.

"'I am sorry but there is nothing I can do to help you,' Mr. Fitzgerald said. 'The will and trust are legally binding.' For a few moments not a word was spoken. As Albert stood up, he looked at Mr. Fitzgerald with infinite dissatisfaction and said, 'I won't be able to accept my wife's decision as it is written in this will. As you know my wife was very ill at the time the original will was revoked. I can easily prove it in court that she was mentally incapable of making any sound decisions.'

"Mr. Fitzgerald apparently anticipated Albert's anger, because he pulled a folder from his briefcase and set it in front of Albert. Inside the folder was evidence of his many extramarital affairs, including many pictures of him with his lovers.

"'Do as you wish, but I suggest reviewing this evidence before taking any legal action,' Mr. Fitzgerald said in a steely voice.

"Inside the folder there was also documentation of Albert's accounting corruptions. Albert hurriedly opened the folder and scanned a few of the items in there. Suddenly his face turned red; he immediately closed the folder and worriedly told Sydney that they should be leaving. They both headed toward the door. Before leaving, Albert, who had just learned that Mr. Fitzgerald's intention would be to make public accusations against him, with a trembling voice said, 'You will hear from my attorney soon.' The two left the office, much to my relief.

"For a moment I felt so strange, as if my heart was laughing. My knees began to shake and I wished Olga could be there to see Albert's volcanic fountains of disappointment and frustration. Albert had at last learned that infidelity has no benefits and Mr. Fitzgerald's hunch proved correct; Albert never filed any law suits against Olga's estate.

"I may sound cruel or thirsty for revenge," Nina told me, drifting back into the present, "but on that day, I felt very proud of Olga. It was courageous, even if she showed it in the last few moments of her life."

A few years after Olga died, Albert left Sydney for another woman, one who was even younger. Nina served as executor of Olga's estate for several years but finally resigned when Albert's anger became too much for her to bear. She also had to deal with Golda and her myriad of problems.

"What happened to the gift trip?" I asked curiously. "Did you ever go to Poland?"

"No," Nina responded, "I didn't."

"After all those years why didn't you use her gift?" I couldn't understand why Nina, who was all about family, culture and her homeland, wouldn't have taken the trip. "Wouldn't traveling to your homeland, especially with your sister, be a great chance now? It may even help Golda's depression!" I exclaimed.

Nina looked at me thoughtfully and said, "I still have my hatred and loathing of those sad childhood memories in Poland. I'm neither ready nor interested in visiting my homeland."

I sensed she didn't want to talk about Poland and dropped the issue, but it always bothered me that she never took the trip.

Chapter Twenty-Five

In 2001, Nina's health condition worsened so suddenly that it was impossible for her to get to Los Angeles from Santa Fe, New Mexico, every two weeks. Instead of visiting Golda, she would speak with her by phone several times a day. In her eighties, dogged by weak eyesight, Nina worked solely on art research and writing appraisals.

The last time I saw her was in October 2001, when she came to Los Angeles to visit Golda. She told me that Golda was taken to the Huntington hospital after suffering a complete mental and physical breakdown. Nina had to rush to Los Angeles and on the phone she told me that Golda was going to receive electric shock treatment.

A few days after she was hospitalized, Golda got well enough to be moved out of the ICU. Nina visited her a few times there and she would sit in a chair, her mind almost blank, hold her sister's hand and talk to her about the beautiful time they used to have when they were children together. I met with Nina, after she had visited Golda in the hospital, in the beautiful Huntington Library gardens.

Nina had dressed all in black again. I was floored with how much Nina had changed since the last I saw her; she was dangerously thin, almost gauntly. It had been almost six months since I had seen her, yet she looked like she aged a lot in that short period of time; she was in the worst health condition that I have ever seen her in. After she arrived, she told me that Golda had undergone extensive treatment for depression. Talking to her, I realized how much she had been deeply affected by the miseries that her sister's illness had brought upon her.

"Have you seen any changes or improvements in her condition after the shock treatment?" I worriedly asked Nina, hoping to hear some good news.

85

"Not really!" Nina sighed. "Nothing, absolutely nothing, has worked on her brain; she has become a mindless creature now. Today I told Golda, 'No matter how many shocks, how many therapies and how much medicine you receive, unless you change your mind to be happy, nothing else can help you, not even God!' But my comments made Golda very angry because she told me that I have no heart or sympathy for her and asked me to leave the room and never come back to see her. So I left the hospital with more stress, sadness and anger.

"No matter how much you love someone," Nina continued, "no matter how close they are to you, if they are making you miserable and causing stress, try to stay away from them. Any negative interactions, such as arguments, blaming, name calling, even eye rolling leads to stress. I was warned by my doctor yesterday of all this as he described the effects of stress." Nina then smiled a bitter smile and said, "He doesn't know that I am now a really miserable person."

I offered to visit Golda while Nina wasn't in town, but again she gave me another excuse for not accepting my offer. We ended up chatting nonstop, but I noted a few times during our conversation that she drifted off and seemed disengaged. Before we said goodbye, I told her that I felt Golda's illness had brought her to a downfall. I suggested taking some time off and going on a trip or doing something with her sister later. She listened to my advice graciously and told me that it was a great idea and that she would do it when Golda was out of the hospital. I then told her that I was going on a trip for three weeks and that I'll call her when I come back.

That day we had the longest talk together. Afterwards, we hugged, kissed and said goodbye. She said that she was going to visit Dianna, her long time friend and confidant, whom I had met a few times in the past.

Chapter Twenty-Six

After returning home from my three week trip to Europe, I called Nina at her home and then the gallery. To my surprise, both numbers were disconnected, which was very unusual for Nina. I thought she might have simply changed her number, but as time passed and I didn't hear from her, I became very worried. I was convinced something must have happened to her or Golda and fired off a letter to Nina's Santa Fe home. I waited anxiously for a week. Still nothing.

I became restless and began searching for the business card Dianna had slipped me the first time I met her. I couldn't find it, so, for the first time, I called the hospital and asked for Golda. I thought she might know where Nina was. To my surprise, the hospital operator told me they didn't have any patient by that name there. I asked a few questions about Golda but they refused to answer. I searched through my apartment again and finally found Dianna's business card. I called Dianna seconds after finding the card, and though we hadn't talked in years, she recognized my voice by the way I said my name.

"I'm worried about Nina," I said anxiously.

"I don't expect you've heard about Nina," Dianna said after a short pause, "but I am very sorry to tell you that she passed away."

Although I suspected something might have happened, the news still came as a terrible shock. My heart lurched and my knees buckled. I began to cry.

As I was trying to control my emotion, I started peppering Dianna with questions. "How did she die? When did she die?" I asked frantically.

"It was quite unexpected," Dianna answered. "She lay down for a little nap at my house in the afternoon and she didn't wake up. It was a peaceful death."

"When?" I sobbed.

"Three days after you left on your trip," Dianna replied.

"That was the last time I saw her," I said, forcing myself to stop crying. "She kept telling me that she had a headache. I thought she didn't look well, and I was so worried about her."

Dianna replied, "Yes, she was very ill. I realized her mind was seriously impaired just before she died. It was as if a dark cloud had settled over her thoughts that week before she passed away. All I feel now is how I'll miss her."

"How did Golda handle the news?" I asked her. "Before I was able to find your number I called the Huntington Hospital but they said she wasn't there. I am very concerned about Golda right now."

Dianna paused for a moment and to my surprise, suggested we talk about Golda in person.

"Is she OK?" I persisted, "Where is she now?" suddenly certain Golda hadn't taken the news of her twin's death very well.

But Dianna didn't answer my questions. All she said was "Thank goodness it is over. Nina had the most dreadful time with her sister. I've never seen anyone like Nina."

"What do you mean?" I asked her, puzzled at her statement.

"Let's get together for lunch this week." Dianna said dismissively, "I've got to run, there's a patient waiting for me." We agreed to meet three days from then at the very restaurant Nina had introduced us at years before.

Three days later, as I was still mourning Nina's death, I met with Dianna around noon. Dianna was an attractive woman, about 80 years old, who had preserved her good looks very well. As we were sitting down at the table, Dianna apologized for that day when she had unexpectedly given me the bad news about Nina's death. She said, "I had been thinking about you after Nina passed away. I meant to call you but I couldn't locate your phone number."

"The day you gave me the news was a terrible day for me," I told her. "I had been so worried about Nina when I returned from my trip, especially when I realized her line had been disconnected. The silence, the worrying, the sleeplessness, they were very anxious moments for me."

"Why didn't you call me first?" Dianna asked.

"I couldn't find your number either," I admitted. "But I was also far too frightened to call you right away because I had a bad feeling something serious may have happened to Nina."

I asked about Golda, no longer able to hold in my burning curiosity. Dianna just listened and didn't say a word as I talked for several minutes about Golda and how I had offered many times to help Nina with her.

"How is Golda doing?" I finally asked.

Dianna just gave me a bitter smile and suggested I finished my lunch first. *Why isn't she answering my questions?* I wondered impatiently to myself.

To cover my agitation, I began talking about Nina and how she'd changed my life from the moment I'd met her many years ago. I told Dianna how Nina had taught me about art, life, and the importance of charity.

As Dianna listened to my description of my friendship with Nina, I sensed some hesitation in her face. Uncertainty had parked itself on her face, as if she was doubtful about telling me something.

"Please, tell me about Golda and Nina," I begged.

"There's so much to say, I don't even know where to start," she said slowly. "I am very sorry that I have to give you this inconvenient truth, the whole truth about Nina and her sister."

My heart dropped to my feet. I was sure Golda had died, too. "Has something happened to Golda?" I cried.

"Yes," Dianna replied. "Golda is dead. You may need to take a deep breath for this."

"Why? What happened?" I was really in a panic; I didn't want to hear more bad news but I needed answers.

"Golda died a long time ago," Dianna said mournfully. Her words rushed through my mind like a burning fuse. I spit out the coffee I had just sipped and sputtered.

"What?" I exclaimed.

"Golda has been dead for 66 years," Dianna revealed. "She died in 1935, during the Holocaust when she was only 19 years old."

The truth hit like a brick on my heart. "This is unbelievable," I sputtered while shaking my head awe.

"I wish I could have told you before," Dianna told me, "but Nina didn't want anyone to know her secret." I just sat there, my head swelling with the bizarreness of Dianna's explanation. I lost my appetite.

"Nina was not just my close friend, she was my long time patient, too," Dianna said. "Did she ever tell you about her friend Olga?"

Olga, it turns out, had introduced Dianna and Nina just a few years before she died of cancer. Shortly after introducing them, Olga told Dianna about Nina's depression; it was then that Dianna also became Nina's psychologist.

"She first became depressed when she was 20," Dianna began to explain. "That was the year she had learned Golda had been killed by Nazis. She complained of violent headaches and hallucinations. It was at that time that the idea of her sister being alive started to flow in her mind."

I gasped, "Unbelievable!"

"I used to think that every year she survived was a miracle, especially with guilt that strong," Dianna commented. "Nina spent the majority of her life living under a hidden quilt of guilt and mental trauma that she suffered because she had survived the Holocaust."

"This is truly the most bizarre thing I've ever heard!" I exclaimed.

"Up until a minute ago," Dianna continued, "I was doubtful about telling you the real truth. But I thought you deserved to know the truth about them."

I pushed my plate away as Dianna went into storyteller mode.

Some of the story I already knew: Nina had told me years before about her parents, how they sometimes violently quarreled and how she and Golda lived with her aunt in Paris after their parents were killed in a car accident. But what I didn't know was that at age 19, Golda, who also was very depressed and ill, was arrested by Nazis. She and several other family members were taken to one of the concentration camps in Poland. Upon their arrival in the camp, all of them were immediately gassed. Nina was living with her aunt in the United States at the time and didn't know the fate of her sister during the war but frantically searched for news. She finally contacted an old neighbor who had settled in Switzerland. It was that neighbor who told Nina that her sister, her uncle, aunt and two small cousins hadn't survived. From then on, Nina struggled with depression for most of her life.

"For the rest of her life," Dianna told me, "Nina wore all black and lived under the shadow of the ghosts of her grief. Reality and fantasy changed places in Nina's memory and preserving her past became a compulsion. She used to bounce from one extreme to another."

My hair stood on end listening to Dianna. I had a hard time believing it, but I knew in my heart that every word was true even if each one was slowly driving me insane. I just kept on listening to Dianna as she went on.

"Nina wanted to believe her sister was still alive so she created an imaginary life for Golda and used every tool in her mind to let the vision of her grow up alongside herself. God knows how many times I warned her that her idea of reality wasn't real at all," Dianna said morosely. "Until she accepted that fact, there was nothing else I could do to help her."

I sat there speechless, still trying to absorb the bizarre truth. There was a commotion in my mind; I didn't know whether it was sadness or madness, whether I should be mad at Nina or to have sympathy for her. The twenty years of friendship, which had always been so sweet, suddenly tasted sour. I felt like I was falling.

At some point during the conversation, Dianna asked if I had ever doubted Nina's story when she was alive. "Never," I told her, "how could I doubt someone who had an incredible sense of ethics and responsibility? Nina and I were best friends and we spent a lot of time together. We shared a cascade of memories and traded ideas at top speed. We were connected by art. We also talked about the Holocaust and our parents but I had no clue about Golda's truth.

"I have to admit that a few times I had become very suspicious and puzzled when Nina strongly refused my offers to help Golda by visiting or calling her.

I sensed something was not right about Golda, and yet I never doubted Nina," I told Dianna reflectively.

"I know you are heartbroken and it is truly weird to hear this," Dianna comforted, "but I hope you understand that the guilt she felt was so strong that it blinded her reality. From treating Nina for years I knew that she suffered from bipolar disorder and I was always terrified that she would go mad. Nevertheless, Golda's story jumped out from her mind when her husband William died. Gradually, she became addicted to the idea that Golda was living by her side. That idea kept her alive until a week before she died."

"What a bitter end for Golda," I said, thinking that for years I had felt sympathetic towards her. "Why would Nina just make up a life for her like that? I really don't understand."

"I think in Nina's case it was the grip of biological forces beyond her control and maybe it was the only way she could go on in her life," Dianna explained.

"But the puzzle that is most intriguing to me," I said, "is how an intelligent person like Nina moves in one direction while feeding her mind a continuous falsehood. I can't figure it out!"

Before Dianna and I said goodbye that day, I thanked her for telling me the truth. She asked, "Knowing what you know now, how do you feel about Nina?"

"I don't know," I said truthfully. "I can't believe it still. My logic is at war with my emotions!"

"I understand. I carried her secret alone for many years," Dianna said.

"All I know is that for the rest of my life I will be wondering who the woman behind these conflicting thoughts and motives was," I replied. "But in all honesty, I am glad she was a part of my life. I shall miss her, and Golda, terribly," I said.

A few years passed after Nina's death and still I heard her low, sweet voice as I painted. When I think about my friends Ziba and Nina, I feel a fuller appreciation for the influence they had on my life and my art, whether it's poetry or painting. I may be able to probe the depths of their mysterious mental states from the perspectives of a philosopher, a psychologist, or a doctor, but no matter what, I can appreciate and understand them. I get on with my life by celebrating theirs.

Afterword

Arriving into this world, everyone has to come face-to-face with the truth about life. What is life? It is a portrait that the mind sees. It can stir up peacefulness, sadness and hope all at once.

Once you discover the significance of the mind, you'll see everything is possible. The mind can serve either the notions of truths or the notions of falsities, it can rearrange our experiences to either improve or destroy life. This is one of the hallmarks of the mind's functions. The vision of the mind brings a revolution in our lives.

Throughout the years, I've learned that each person sees things differently in the mind's reverberation. One's reflections on pain, grief, love, friendship, faith, and inner relationship differ than another's. We stick with our inner voice until we see either a harvest or devastation in our lives; it depends on how our minds see the portrait of our lives.

I decided to write this book to share the story of my friendship with two women in my life. The human psyche is no doubt significant and it is apparent in this book where I stand when I explore the power of the mind. The mind tells us, this is our life; this is the way it's going to be, be it blissful or turbulent.

It was through these two friends that I learned this: if destiny chooses you, or, if you choose density, you must move on with your life because it is movement that ignites your inner fire and energy. When you accept life as it is, you begin to enjoy it like never before. For these two friends, life was something that they had chosen to accomplish! They proved that the human condition isn't desolate if the human spirit is present. Share your heart's desire with your mind, apply your most vivid imaginations, only then joy is possible and life will work. This is the true essence of life!